HEAVEN IN DISORDER

HEAVEN IN DISORDER

SLAVOJ ŽIŽEK

OR Books

New York · London

All rights information: rights@orbooks.com
Visit our website at www.orbooks.com

First printing 2021

Published by OR Books, New York and London

Library of Congress Cataloging-in-Publication Data: A catalog record for this book is available from the Library of Congress.

Typeset by Lapiz Digital Services.

paperback ISBN 978-1-68219-281-8 • ebook ISBN 978-1-68219-285-6

CONTENTS

INTRODUCTION:
IS THE SITUATION STILL EXCELLENT?

One of Mao Zedong's best-known sayings is: "There is great disorder under heaven; the situation is excellent." It is easy to understand what Mao meant here: when the existing social order is disintegrating, the ensuing chaos offers revolutionary forces a great chance to act decisively and take political power. Today, there certainly is great disorder under heaven, with the Covid-19 pandemic, global warming, signs of a new Cold War, and the eruption of popular protests and social antagonisms worldwide naming but a few of the crises that beset us. But does this chaos still make the situation excellent, or is the danger of self-destruction too high? The difference between the situation that Mao had in mind and our own situation can be best rendered by a tiny terminological distinction. Mao speaks about disorder *under* heaven, wherein "heaven," or the big Other in whatever form—the inexorable logic of historical processes, the laws of social development—still exists and discreetly regulates social chaos. Today, we should talk about *heaven itself* as being in disorder. What do I mean by this?

In *Divided Heaven* (1963), Christa Wolf's classic GDR novel about the subjective impact of divided Germany, Manfred (who has chosen the West) says to his love, Rita, when they meet for the last time: "But even if our land is divided, we still share the same heaven." Rita (who has chosen to remain in the East) bitterly replies: "No, they first divided the heaven." Apologetic (of the East) as the novel is, it offers the right insight into how our "earthly" divisions and fights are ultimately always grounded in a "divided heaven"; that is, in a much more radical and exclusive division of the very (symbolic) universe in which we dwell. The bearer and instrument of this "division of heaven" is language as the medium that sustains the way we experience reality—language, not primitive egotistic interests, is the first and greatest divider. It is because of language that we (can) "live in different worlds" to our neighbors, even when they live on the same street.

Today, the situation is not one in which heaven is divided into two spheres, as was the case in the Cold War period when two global world-views confronted each other. The divisions of heaven today appear increasingly drawn within each particular country. In the United States, for instance, there is an ideological and political civil war between the alt-Right and the liberal-democratic establishment, while in the United Kingdom there are similarly deep divisions, as were recently expressed in the opposition between Brexiteers and anti-Brexiteers . . . Spaces for common ground are ever diminishing, mirroring the ongoing enclosure of physical public space, and this is happening at a time when multiple intersecting crises mean that global solidarity and international cooperation are more needed than ever.

In recent months, the often alarming ways in which the crisis of the Covid-19 pandemic is intertwined with ongoing social, political, ecological, and economic crises are increasingly apparent. The pandemic must be treated together with global warming, erupting class antagonisms, patriarchy and misogyny, and the many other ongoing crises that resonate with it, and with each other, in a complex interplay. This interplay is uncontrollable and full of dangers, and we cannot count on any guarantee in heaven to make the solution clearly imaginable. Such a risky situation makes our moment an eminently political one: the situation is decidedly *not* excellent, and that's why one has to act.

Slavoj Žižek

What, then, is to be done? Lenin's demand for a "concrete analysis of the concrete situation" is today more actual than ever. No simple universal formula can provide the answer—there are moments in which pragmatic support for modest progressive measures is needed; there are moments when a radical confrontation is the only way; and there are moments when a sobering silence (and a cute pair of mittens) speak more than a thousand words.

1.

WAS THE DRONE ATTACK ON SAUDI ARABIA REALLY A GAME CHANGER?

When, in September of 2019, the Houthi rebels from Yemen launched a drone attack on Saudi Aramco's crude-oil processing facilities, our media repeatedly characterized this event as a "game changer"—but was it really? In some common sense yes, since it perturbed the global oil supply and increased the likelihood of a large armed conflict in the Middle East. However, one should be careful not to miss the cruel irony of this claim.

Houthi rebels in Yemen have been in an open war with Saudi Arabia for years, and Saudi armed forces (supplied by the United States and the United Kingdom) have practically destroyed the entire country, indiscriminately bombing civilian objects. The Saudi intervention led to one of the worst humanitarian catastrophes, with tens of thousands of children dead. But, as was the case with Libya and Syria, destroying an entire country is here obviously not a game changer but part of the normal geopolitical game.

Even if we condemn the Houthi act, should we really be surprised to see the Houthis, cornered and in a desperate situation, striking back in whatever way they can? Far from changing the game, their act is its logical culmination. To paraphrase one of Donald Trump's unspeakable vulgarities, they finally found the way to grab Saudi Arabia by its p****, where it really hurts. Or, to paraphrase the famous line from

Brecht's *Beggar's Opera*, "What is robbing a bank compared to founding a new bank": what is destroying a country compared to slightly disturbing the reproduction of capital?

The media attention grabbed by the "game-changing" Houthi attack also conveniently distracted us from other truly game-changing projects, like the Israeli plan to annex large fertile chunks of the West Bank.[1] What this meant is that all the talk about the two-state solution was just that, empty talk meant to obfuscate the ruthless realization of a modern-day colonization project in which what awaits the West Bank Palestinians will be, in the best case scenario, a couple of tightly controlled Bantustans. One should also note that Israel is doing this with the silent connivance of Saudi Arabia—a further proof that a new axis of evil is emerging in the Middle East composed of Saudi Arabia, Israel, Egypt, and the United Arab Emirates. It is here that the rules of the game are truly changing!

And, to broaden the scope of our analysis, one should also be attentive to how the game is changing with the Hong Kong protests. A dimension that is as a rule ignored in our media is the class struggle which sustains the Hong Kong protests against China's efforts to constrain its autonomy. The Hong Kong protests first erupted in poor districts; the rich were prospering under Chinese control. Then a new voice was heard. On September 8, 2019, protesters marched to the US consulate in Hong Kong, with CNN reporting that "One banner carried at the march read 'President Trump, please liberate Hong Kong' in English, [while] some marchers sang the US national anthem."[2] Thirty-year-old banker David Wong was reported as saying:

1 Oliver Holmes, "Netanyahu Vows to Annex Large Parts of the Occupied West Bank," the *Guardian*, September 11, 2019, https://www.theguardian.com/world/2019/sep/10/netanyahu-vows-annex-large-parts-occupied-west-bank-trump.

2 Ben Westcott, Julia Hollingsworth, and Caitlin Hu, "Hong Kong Protesters March to US Consulate to Call for Help From Trump," CNN, September 9, 2019, https://edition.cnn.com/2019/09/08/asia/hong-kong-us-protests-0809-intl-hnk/index.html.

"We share the same US values of liberty and democracy." Every serious analysis of the Hong Kong protests has to focus on how a social protest, potentially a true game changer, was recuperated into the standard narrative of the democratic revolt against totalitarian rule. And the same goes for analysis of Mainland China itself, with our media reporting on how the Unirule Institute of Economics, one of China's few remaining outposts of liberal thought, has been ordered to shut down, in what is seen as another sign of the dramatically shrinking space for public debate under the government of the Chinese leader, Xi Jinping. However, this is far from the police intimidation, beatings, and arrests to which leftist students in China are being submitted. Ironically taking the official return to Marxism more seriously than it was meant, groups of students have organized links with workers who suffer extreme exploitation in factories around Beijing. In chemical factories especially, pollution is extreme, largely uncontrolled, and ignored by state power, and students help workers to organize themselves and formulate their demands. Such links between students and workers pose the true challenge to the regime, while the struggle between the new hard line of Xi Jinping and the pro-capitalist liberals is ultimately part of the dominant game. It expresses the dominant tension between the two versions of unbridled capitalist development: authoritarian and liberal.

In all these cases, from Yemen to China, one should thus learn to distinguish between the conflicts which are part of the game and the true game changers which are either ominous turns for the worse masked as the continuation of the normal state of things (Israel annexing large parts of the West Bank), or hopeful signs of something really new emerging. The predominant liberal view is obsessed by the first and largely ignores the second.

2.

WHO MAKES KURDISTAN WILD?

Well over a hundred years ago, Karl May wrote a bestseller, *Through Wild Kurdistan*, about the adventures of a German hero, Kara Ben Nemsi, in that part of the world. This immensely popular book helped to construct in central Europe a perception of Kurdistan as a place of brutal tribal warfare, naïve honesty, and honor, but also of superstition, betrayal, and permanent cruel warfare—the almost caricatural barbaric Other of European civilization. If we look at today's Kurdistan, we cannot but be surprised by the extent to which it contrasts with this cliché. When I was in Turkey, where I know the situation relatively well, I noticed that the Kurdish minority is the most modern and secular part of society, at a distance from every religious fundamentalism and with a developed feminism.

When, in October 2019, Donald Trump endorsed the Turkish attack on the Kurdish enclave in northern Syria, the self-designated "stable genius" justified his betrayal of the Kurds by noting that the Kurds are "no angels."[3] For him, of course, the only angels in that region are Israel (especially in the West Bank) and Saudi Arabia (especially in Yemen). However, in some sense, the Kurds *are* the only angels in that part of the world. The fate of the Kurds makes them the exemplary

3 Philip Bump, "Trump's Indifferent to New Fighting in Syria: 'There's a Lot of Sand There That They Can Play With,'" the *Washington Post*, October 16, 2019, https://www.washingtonpost.com/politics/2019/10/16/trumps-indifferent-new-fighting-syria-theres-lot-sand-there-that-they-can-play-with/.

victim of the ongoing geopolitical colonial games: spread along the borderline of four neighboring states (Turkey, Syria, Iraq, Iran), their (more than deserved) full autonomy was in nobody's interest, and they paid the full price for it. Do we still remember Saddam Hussein's mass bombing and gas-poisoning of Kurds in the north of Iraq in the late 1980s? More recently, for years, Turkey has played a well-planned military–political game, officially fighting ISIS but actually bombing the Kurds who are really fighting ISIS.

In recent decades, the ability of the Kurds to organize their communal life was tested in almost clear-cut experimental conditions. The moment they were given a space to breathe freely outside the conflicts of the states around them, they surprised the world. After the fall of Saddam, the Kurdish enclave in northern Iraq developed into the only safe part of Iraq, with well-functioning institutions and even regular flights to Europe. In northern Syria, the Kurdish enclave centered in Rojava was a unique place in today's geopolitical mess. When the Kurds were given a respite from the constant threats of their big neighbors, they quickly built a society that one cannot but designate an actually existing and well-functioning utopia. Through my own professional interest, I noticed the thriving intellectual community in Rojava, where I was repeatedly invited to give lectures (these plans were brutally interrupted by military tensions in the area).

But what especially saddened me was the reaction of some of my "leftist" colleagues who were bothered by the fact that the Kurds had to rely on US military protection. What should they have done, caught as they were in the tensions between Turkey, the Syrian civil war, the Iraqi mess, and Iran? Did they have any other choice? Should they have sacrificed themselves on the altar of anti-imperialist solidarity? This "leftist" critical distance was no less disgusting than that shown in 2018, when an agreement was reached between Greece and the Republic of Macedonia to resolve the dispute over the latter's name. The solution, which was for Macedonia to change its name to North Macedonia, was instantly attacked by radicals in both countries. Greek opponents insisted that "Macedonia" is an old Greek name, and Macedonian opponents felt humiliated by being reduced to a "northern" province when they are the only people who call themselves "Macedonians." Imperfect as it was, this solution offered a glimpse of an end to a long and meaningless struggle through a reasonable compromise. But it was caught in another "contradiction": the struggle between big powers (the United States and European Union on the one side, and Russia on the other). The West put pressure on both sides to accept the compromise so that Macedonia could quickly join the EU and NATO, while, for essentially the same reason (fearing a loss of influence in the Balkans), Russia opposed it, supporting rabid conservative nationalist forces in both countries. So which side should we take here? I think we should decidedly take the side of the compromise, for the simple reason that it is the only realist solution to the problem. Supporting Russia here would mean sacrificing a reasonable solution to the singular problem of Macedonian and Greek relations to international geopolitical interests. Will the Kurds be dealt the same blow from our anti-imperialist "leftists"?

That's why it is our duty to fully support the Kurdish resistance to the Turkish invasion, and to rigorously denounce the dirty games being played by Western powers. While the sovereign states around them are gradually sinking into a new barbarism, the Kurds are the only glimmer of hope. And this struggle does not only concern the Kurds but also ourselves and the shape of the emerging global new order. If the Kurds are abandoned, a new order will emerge in which there will be no place for the precious European legacy of emancipation. If Europe turns its eyes away from the Kurds, it will betray itself and become a true Europastan!

3.

TROUBLES IN OUR PARADISE

In mid-October 2019, Chinese media launched an offensive promoting the claim that "demonstrations in Europe and South America are the direct result of Western tolerance of Hong Kong unrest."[4] In a commentary published in *Beijing News*, former Chinese diplomat Wang Zhen wrote that "the disastrous impact of a 'chaotic Hong Kong' has begun to influence the Western world," i.e., that demonstrators in Chile and Spain were taking their cues from Hong Kong. Along the same lines, an editorial in *Global Times* accused Hong Kong demonstrators of "exporting revolution to the world," claiming that "The West is paying the price for supporting riots in Hong Kong, which has quickly kindled violence in other parts of the world and foreboded the political risks that the West can't manage."[5] In a video editorial posted to the *Global Times* official Twitter, editor Hu Xijin said, "There are many problems in the West and all kinds of undercurrents of dissatisfaction. Many of them will eventually manifest in the way the Hong Kong protests did."[6] And the ominous conclusion: "Catalonia is probably just the beginning."

4 See Ben Westcott, "West Is Paying the Price For Supporting Hong Kong Riots, Chinese State Media Says," CNN, October 22 2019, https://edition.cnn .com/2019/10/21/asia/china-hong-kong-chile-spain-protests-intl-hnk/index.html.

5 "HK-Style Violence to Impact Western System," *Global Times*, October 20, 2019, https://www.globaltimes.cn/content/1167409.shtml.

6 Westcott, "West Is Paying the Price For Supporting Hong Kong Riots."

Although the idea that demonstrations in Barcelona and Chile are taking their cues from Hong Kong is far-fetched, this is not to say that these outbursts—in Hong Kong, Catalonia, Chile, Ecuador, and Lebanon, not to mention the *gilets jaunes* in France—cannot be reduced to a common denominator. In each of the cases, a protest against a particular law or measure (higher fuel prices in France, the extradition law in Hong Kong, the rise of public transport fares in Chile, long prison terms for pro-independence Catalonian politicians in Barcelona, etc.) exploded into a general discontent that was obviously already there, lurking and waiting for a contingent trigger to detonate it. This meant that even when the particular law or measure was repealed, the protests persisted.

Two weird facts cannot but strike the eye here. First, the way that "communist" China discreetly plays on the solidarity of those in power all around the world against the rebellious populace, warning the West not to underestimate the dissatisfaction in their own countries. China's message here is that, beneath all the ideological and geopolitical tensions, all states share the same basic interest in holding onto power. Second is the "trouble in paradise" aspect: protests are not taking place in poor, desolate countries but in countries of (relative, at least) prosperity, countries that are typically presented as (economic, at least) success stories. Although these protests indicate growing inequalities that belie the official success story, they cannot be reduced to economic issues. The dissatisfaction they express indicates the growing (normative) expectations of how our societies should function, expectations that also concern "non-economic" issues like collective or individual freedoms, dignity, even meaningful life. Something that was till recently accepted as normal (a certain degree of poverty, full state sovereignty, etc.) is increasingly perceived as a wrong to be combatted.

This is why we should also include in the series of ongoing protests the new explosion of ecological movements and feminist struggle (the true one, the one that involves thousands of ordinary women, not its sanitized American MeToo version). Let's just focus on one case. In Mexico, the massive feminist mobilization involves what organizer Alejandra Santillana Ortiz calls "the conversation about life, dignified life and rage."[7] She continues: "What does life mean for us? What are we referring to when we speak of putting life at the center? For us, life is not a declarative abstract, it necessarily involves talking about dignity and everything that makes it possible to enable dignity." We are not talking here about abstract philosophical speculations on the meaning of life, but about reflections rooted in concrete experiences that prove how the most ordinary activities of daily life—things like taking a subway—are rife with dangers of brutal violence and humiliation:

How can a person have peace of mind knowing that on the metro in Mexico City, an integral part of the commute in the city, thousands of women have been kidnapped in a matter of months and that this all took place in public and in broad daylight? And if you aren't kidnapped, you must consider the very high probability that you will be assaulted, or that you will encounter a violent aggression of some kind. This is the reason why there are there separate women-only cars on trains, but even then there are men who get on these cars.

Mexico may be an extreme case here, but it is just an extrapolation of the tendencies found everywhere. We live in societies in which brutal male violence boils just beneath the surface, and one thing is clear: political correctness is not the way to beat it. What also makes Mexico exemplary is the secret solidarity between this persisting male

7 Alejandra Santillana Ortiz, interview by Tobias Boos, "Graffiti and Glitter Bombs: Mexico's Movement Against Rape," *New Frame*, October 23, 2019 https://www .newframe.com/graffiti-and-glitter-bombs-mexicos-movement-against-rape/.

brutality and the state apparatuses that we expect to protect us from it. As Santillana Ortiz says:

There is a kind of formation of a violent society without punishment in which the state is part of that violence. A great many of the crimes that have been committed in recent years in Mexico have the state and its functionaries or the police directly involved. Or, through judges or those in the justice system, the state guarantees generalized impunity in this country.

The terrifying vision of "generalized impunity" is the truth of the new wave of populism, and only vast popular mobilization is strong enough to confront this obscene complicity of state and civil society. This is why the ongoing protests around the world express a growing dissatisfaction that cannot be channeled into established modes of political representation. However, we should avoid at any cost celebrating these protests for their distance toward established politics. Here, a difficult "Leninist" task lies ahead: how to organize the growing dissatisfaction in all its forms, including the ecological and feminist protests, into a large-scale coordinated movement. If we fail in this, what awaits us are societies of permanent states of exception and civil unrest.

4.

THE DANGERS OF SHARING A CUP OF COFFEE WITH ASSANGE

On Thursday, November 21, 2019, I visited Julian Assange in Belmarsh prison, and one small detail, insignificant in itself, struck me as emblematic of the way that prisons respectful of our (visitors' and prisoners') welfare and human rights function. All the guards were very kind and repeatedly emphasized that everything they do is for our own good. For example, even though Assange has now served his time and remains in prison under protective custody, he is in solitary confinement twenty-three hours per day, he has to eat all his meals alone in his cell, when he is allowed to go out for one hour he cannot meet other prisoners, and the communication with a guard who accompanies him is reduced to minimum—why this severe treatment? The explanation I was given was a predictable one: it is for his own good (since he is a traitor hated by many, he may be attacked if he mixes with other people . . .). But the craziest case of this care for "our good" happened when Assange's assistant who accompanied me brought me a cup of coffee, which was put onto a table where Julian and I were sitting. I took the plastic lid off the cup, took a sip, and then put the cup back on the table without putting the lid back on; immediately (in two or three seconds) a guard approached me and signaled to me with a hand gesture (very kindly, it is a humanist prison if ever there was one) that I should put the lid back on the cup of coffee. I did as I was told, but I was slightly surprised by the demand and, when leaving the prison, I asked some of the personnel what the reason was. The explanation was again, of course, a warm human one—something like: "It is for your own good and protection, sir. You were sitting at a table with a dangerous prisoner probably prone to violent acts, and seeing between the two of you an open cup of hot coffee . . ." I felt warmth in my heart at being so well protected—just imagine to what threat I might have been exposed if I were visiting Assange in a Russian or Chinese prison; the guards would undoubtedly ignore this noble safety measure and expose me to a terrible danger!

My visit took place a couple of days after Sweden dropped its own demand for Assange's extradition, clearly admitting, after further interrogation of witnesses, that there were no grounds for prosecution. However, this decision was not without an ominous background. When there are two demands for a person's extradition, a judge has to decide which comes first, and if Sweden was chosen then this might jeopardize the US extradition (it can be delayed, public opinion may turn against it . . .). Now, with only the United States asking for extradition, the situation is much clearer.

So now is the time to ask the elementary question: did Sweden really need eight years to question a couple of witnesses and thus establish Assange's innocence (ruining his life in this long period and contributing to his character assassination)? Now that it is clear that the rape accusations were a lie, neither the Swedish state organs nor the British press engaged in Assange's character assassination had the decency to offer a clear apology. Where are all those journalists who wrote that Assange should be extradited to Sweden instead of the United States? Or, incidentally, those who babbled that Assange was paranoiac, that there was no extradition awaiting him, that if he left the Ecuadorian embassy he would be free after a couple of weeks in prison, that all he had to fear was fear itself? This last claim is for me a kind of negative proof of God's inexistence: if there was a just God, then lightning would strike the author of this obscene paraphrase of F. D. Roosevelt's famous quip from the time of the Great Depression.

Since I already mentioned China, I cannot restrain myself from reminding readers what triggered the large protests in Hong Kong that have been going on for months: China's demand that Hong Kong accepts the law that will compel Hong Kong authorities to extradite its citizens to China when China demands it. It now seems to me that the United Kingdom is more subservient to the United States than Hong Kong is to China: the British government sees nothing problematic in extraditing a person accused of a political crime to the United States. China's demand is even more justified since Hong Kong is ultimately part of China, the formula being "one country, two systems." Obviously, the relationship between the United Kingdom and the United States is "two countries, one system" (the American one, of course). Brexit is promoted as a means to assert British sovereignty, and now, apropos Assange, we can already see what this sovereignty amounts to—subservience to US demands.

Now is the time for all honest Brexiteers to staunchly oppose Assange's extradition. We are no longer dealing with a minor legal or political matter, but with something that concerns the basic meaning of our freedom and human rights. When will the broad public understand that the story of Assange is the story of themselves, that their own fate will be deeply affected by whether or not he is extradited? We should help Julian not out of some vague humanitarian concern and sympathy for a miserable victim, but out of a concern for our own future.

5.

ANATOMY OF A COUP: DEMOCRACY, THE BIBLE, AND LITHIUM

Although I have been a staunch supporter of Evo Morales for over a decade, I must admit that, after reading about the confusion after Morales's disputed 2019 electoral victory, I was beset by doubts: Did he also succumb to the authoritarian temptation, as has happened to so many radical leftists in power? However, after a day or two, things became clear.

Brandishing a giant leather-bound Bible and declaring herself Bolivia's interim president, Jeanine Añez, the second vice president of the Senate, declared: "The Bible has returned to the government palace."[8] She added: "We want to be a democratic tool of inclusion and unity." Yet the transitional cabinet sworn into office did not include a single Indigenous person. This says it all: although the majority of Bolivia's population are Indigenous or mixed race, they were, till the rise of Morales, de facto excluded from political life, reduced to the silent majority who do society's dirty work in the shadows. What happened with Morales was the political awakening of this silent majority who did not fit into the network of capitalist relations. They were not yet proletarian in the modern sense; they remained immersed

8 Nathan J. Robinson, "Lessons from the Bolivian Coup," *Current Affairs*, November 26, 2019, https://www.currentaffairs.org/2019/11/lessons-from-the-bolivian-coup.

in their premodern tribal social identities. Here is how Álvaro García Linera, Morales's vice president, described their lot:[9]

"In Bolivia, food was produced by Indigenous farmers, buildings and houses were built by Indigenous workers, streets were cleaned by Indigenous people, and the elite and the middle classes entrusted the care of their children to them. Yet the traditional left seemed oblivious to this and occupied itself only with workers in large-scale industry, paying no attention to their ethnic identity."

To understand Bolivia's Indigenous people, we should bring into the picture the entire historical weight of their predicament: they are the survivors of perhaps the greatest holocaust in the history of humanity, their communities obliterated with the Spanish and English colonization of the Americas.

The religion of Bolivia's Indigenous people is a unique combination of Catholicism and belief in the Pachamama, or Mother Earth figure. This is why, although Morales stated that he is a Catholic, in the current Bolivian constitution (enacted in 2009) the Roman Catholic church lost its official status. Its article IV states: "The State respects and guarantees freedom of religion and spiritual beliefs, according to their view of the world. The State is independent of religion." And it is against such affirmations of Indigenous culture that Añez's display of the Bible is directed. The message is clear: an open assertion of white religious supremacism, and a no less open attempt to put the silent majority back in their proper subordinate place. From his Mexican exile, Morales appealed to the Pope to intervene, and the latter's reaction will tell us a lot. Will Francis react as a true Christian and unambiguously reject the enforced re-Catholicization of Bolivia for what

9 Álvaro García Linera, interview by Marcello Musto, "Bolivian Vice President Álvaro García Linera on Marx and Indigenous Politics," *Truthout*, November 9, 2019, https://truthout.org/articles/bolivian-vice-president-alvaro-garcia-linera-on-marx -and-indigenous-politics/.

it is, a political power-play which betrays the emancipatory core of Christianity?

If we leave aside the possible role of lithium in the coup (Bolivia has big reserves of the resource, needed for batteries in electric cars), the big question is: why is Bolivia such a thorn in the flesh of the Western liberal establishment? The answer is a very peculiar one: the surprising fact that the political awakening of premodern tribalism in Bolivia did not result in a new version of the Sendero Luminoso or Khmer Rouge horror show. The reign of Morales was not the usual story of the radical Left in power screwing things up economically and politically, generating poverty and trying to maintain power through authoritarian measures. A proof of the non-authoritarian character of the Morales reign is that he didn't purge the army and police of his opponents (which is why they turned against him).

Morales and his followers were, of course, not perfect; they made mistakes, there were conflicts of interests in his movement. However, the overall balance is an outstanding one. Morales is not Chavez; hedid not have oil money to quell problems, so his government had to engage in the hard and patient work of solving problems in the poorest country in Latin America. The result was nothing short of a miracle: the economy thrived, the poverty rate fell, and health care improved, while all the democratic institutions so dear to liberals continued to function. The Morales government maintained a delicate balance between Indigenous forms of communal activity and modern politics, fighting simultaneously for tradition and women's rights.

To tell the entire story of the coup in Bolivia, we need a whistleblower to reveal the relevant documents. What is evident is that Morales, Linera, and their followers were such a thorn in the flesh of the liberal establishment precisely because they succeeded: for over a decade the radical Left was in power and Bolivia did not turn into Cuba or Venezuela. Democratic socialism is possible.

6.

CHILE: TOWARD A NEW SIGNIFIER

Nicol Barria-Asenjo and Slavoj Žižek

Two recent events have raised some hope in our depressive times: the elections in Bolivia and the APRUEBO referendum in Chile. In Bolivia, the party of Evo Morales returned to power, with Lucho Arce, the minister of economy in Morales's years, triumphantly elected as a new president. On October 25, 2020, Chilean voters were asked to choose between "apruebo"—approving the change of the constitution in the direction of more social justice and freedoms—and "rechazo," rejecting this change. In both cases, we have a rare overlapping of "formal" democracy (free elections) with a substantial people's will. While what happened in Bolivia is different from what is going on in Chile, I hope both share the same long-term outcome.

The events in Bolivia and Chile prove that, in spite of all ideological manipulations, even so-called "bourgeois democracy" can sometimes work. However, liberal democracy is today reaching its limits—in order to work, it has to be supplemented with . . . what? Something very interesting is now emerging in France as a reaction to the public's massive mistrust in state institutions: a rebirth of local citizens' assemblies first practiced by the Ancient Greeks. As Peter Yeung writes in the *Guardian*:

as far back as 621BC the ecclesia, or popular assembly of ancient Athens was a forum in which any male citizen regardless of class could participate. Now, with a pandemic-induced economic and social crisis looming, this ancient democratic tool is being updated for the 21st century. Towns, cities and regions across France are increasingly turning to their citizens to help steer them towards a more egalitarian future.[10]

These forums are not organized by local state apparatuses, they are self-organized by active members of local communities outside the state and involve a strong element of chance, of lottery. The number of randomly selected delegates is 150. We find a vaguely similar procedure in Chile after the victory of the APRUEBO referendum, where 155 individuals were selected from outside the institutional political forces to work on the draft of a new constitution.

Mark Twain supposedly said: "If voting made any difference, they wouldn't let us do it." There are no proofs that he really did say or write this—its most probable origin is a 1976 newspaper column by Robert S. Borden in the *Lowell Sun*. Writing about the US electoral system, Borden wrote: "Has it ever dawned on the editors that the attitudes of the 70 million projected non-voters may be very consistent with the reality that the concept of voting and electing representatives is basically dishonest and fraudulent. If voting could change anything it would be made illegal!"[11] However, the claim is attributed to Twain for good reason: it faithfully reflects his stance. Although Twain was

10 Peter Yeung, "It Gave Me Hope in Democracy': How French Citizens Are Embracing People Power," the *Guardian*, November 20, 2020, https://www .theguardian.com/world/2020/nov///20/it-gave-me-hope-in-democracy-how -french-citizens-are-embracing-people-power.

11 "Quote on Voting Doesn't Tally as Mark Twain," AAP FactCheck, December 19, 2019, https://factcheck.aap.com.au/social-media-claims/quote-on-voting-doesnt -tally-as-mark-twain.

an advocate of voting rights for everybody (women included) and solicited people to vote, he was deeply skeptical about the machinations that prevent the majority from expressing their will. One should accept the quoted thesis in principle, as universally valid—but one should ground this universality in an exception. From time to time, on rare occasions, there *are* elections and referendums which *do* matter. Although these elections are the only ones that deserve to be characterized as "democratic," they are as a rule interpreted as a sign of instability, as an indication that democracy is in danger.

The coup against the Morales regime in Bolivia legitimized itself as a return to parliamentary "normality" against the "totalitarian" danger that Morales would abolish democracy and turn Bolivia into a new Cuba or Venezuela. The truth was that, in the decade of Morales's reign, Bolivia did establish a successful new "normality," bringing together democratic mobilization of the people with clear economic progress. As their new president, Lucho Arce, Morales's minister of economy, pointed out, in the decade of Morales's reign Bolivians enjoyed the best years of their lives. It was the coup against Morales that destroyed this hard-won normality and brought new chaos and misery. With the electoral victory of Arce, therefore, Bolivia doesn't have to begin from a zero-point—it is enough for it to just return to the state of things before the coup and go on from there.

In Chile, the situation is more complex. October is a Chilean month, a month in which radical turns in the country's political history take place. It was on October 24, 1970, that Salvador Allende's victory was ratified; on October 18, 2019, wide popular protests announcing the end of the Pinochet normalization exploded; and on October 25, 2020 (incidentally, the very date of the October Revolution according to the old Russian calendar), the victory of APRUEBO took place which brought with it the disappearance from public space of the symbols associated with the Pinochet era. October is thus not just another month in the Chilean calendar; it is deeply associated with historical and symbolic ruptures that the people decided to undertake.

Although respecting all formal-democratic rules, Allende enforced a series of measures which were perceived as way too "radical" by the ruling class. With active support from the United States, the ruling class organized a series of economic sabotages, and when even this didn't diminish popular support for Allende, his government was overthrown by a military coup d'état on September 11, 1973 (the *true* catastrophe of 9/11). After four years of pure military dictatorship, in 1977 the creation of the Political Constitution of Chile was entrusted to the "Commission of Studies of the New Constitution," formed of twelve people appointed by the Military Junta. The draft drawn up by this group was modified by the Council of State, also designated by the Junta, and finally by General Pinochet himself. The purpose of this document was to ensure the survival of the model that was being implemented in the country, leaving the capacity for future freedom suspended with respect to economic decisions that could threaten such a model.

Pinochet thus enforced his own "democratic" normalization with the new constitution which safely secured the privileges of the rich within a neoliberal order. The protests that erupted in October 2019 are a proof that the Pinochet democratization was a fake, as is every democracy tolerated or even promoted by a dictatorial power. The APRUEBO movement that grew out of these protests wisely focused on the change of constitution. It made it clear to the majority of Chileans that the democratic normalization coordinated by Pinochet was a continuation of the Pinochet regime by other means: the Pinochet forces remained in the background as the "deep state" making sure that the democratic game didn't run out of control. Now that the illusion of Pinochet's democratic normalization is broken, the real hard work lies ahead. In contrast to Bolivia, Chile doesn't have an already established order to return to, so it will have to carefully build a new normality for which even the glorious Allende years cannot really serve as a model.

There are dangers on this path. The electoral victory is only the beginning; the real hard work begins the day after, when the enthusiasm is over and the new normality of a post-capitalist world has to be patiently constructed. In weeks and months to come, the people of Chile will often hear from their enemies the eternal question: "OK, now that you've won, could you tell us precisely what you want? Could you clearly define your project?" The answer is perhaps indicated by the old joke from the United States about an experienced woman who wants to introduce an idiot to sex. She undresses him, masturbates him a little bit, and after he gets an erection, spreads her legs and directs his penis into her vagina. Then she tells him: "OK, we are there, now you just move your penis a little bit out and then deep in again, out and in, out and in . . ." After a minute or so, the idiot explodes in fury: "Can't you finally decide—is it in or out?!"

Those who will criticize Chile will act exactly like this idiot: they will demand a clear decision on what new form of society is wanted. But the victory of APRUEBO is obviously not the end, the conclusion of a struggle; it is the beginning of a long and difficult process to construct a new post-Pinochet normality, a process with many improvisations and steps back and forward. In a way this struggle will be more difficult than the protests and campaign for APRUEBO. The campaign had a clear enemy and just had to articulate the injustices and misery caused by the enemy, with the emancipatory goals in comfortable abstraction: dignity, social and economic justice, etc. Now APRUEBO has to operationalize its program, to translate it into a series of concrete measures, and this will bring out all the internal differences that are ignored in the ecstatic solidarity of the people. (To return to our obscene joke, the people of Chile should treat their opponents exactly like the sexual idiot should be treated, telling them: "No, we began a long and joyful process where there is no quick conclusion, and we will slowly go in and out, in and out, till the moment when the Chilean people are fully satisfied!")

Threats to the emancipatory process are already appearing. As expected, some rightists try to appropriate the discourse of social democracy against the APRUEBO "extremists." Within APRUEBO itself, there are signs of a conflict between those who want to remain within the traditional representative democracy and those who want a more radical social mobilization. The way out of this predicament is not to get stuck in boring "principled" debates but to get to work, elaborate and enforce different projects. Daniel Jadue is the right person to coordinate these efforts, especially considering his achievements as the mayor of Recoleta. The great hit of the Chilean group Los Prisioneros, "El Baile de Los Que Sobran" ("The Dance of Those Who Are Left Over"), became the musical symbol of the protesters occupying the streets. Now Chile needs *el trabajo duro de los que sobran* (the hard work of those who are left over). If this does not happen, the old regime will survive with a new social-democratic mask, and the tragedy of 1973 (the coup against Allende) will repeat itself as a postmodern cynical farce.

It is too risky to predict how this struggle will end. The main obstacle is not the legacy of Pinochet as such but the legacy of the gradual (fake) opening of his dictatorial regime. Especially through the 1990s, Chilean society underwent what we may call a fast post-modernization: an explosion of consumerist hedonism, superficial sexual permissiveness, competitive individualism, and so on. Those in power realized that such atomized social space is much more effective than direct state oppression against radical leftist projects which rely on social solidarity: classes continue to exist "in themselves" but not "for themselves"; I see others from my class more as competitors than as members of a same group with solidarity interests. Direct state oppression tends to unite opposition and promote organized forms of resistance, while in "postmodern" societies even extreme dissatisfaction assumes the form of chaotic revolts which soon run out of breath, unable to reach the "Leninist" stage of an organized force with a clear program.[12]

What gives some hope in Chile is a series of specific features, suffice it to mention just two. First is the strong political engagement of psychoanalysts, predominantly Lacanians, on the Left side—they played a strong role in the protests that erupted in October of 2019, plus in the organization that led to the victory of APRUEBO in the referendum. Second, in Chile (as in some other countries like Bolivia, but in contrast to Brazil) the new rightist populism never successfully caught on; the popular mobilization has a clear leftist character. Are these two features somehow connected?

Where does psychoanalysis stand with regard to radical social change? It mostly occupies a "moderate" liberal place and worries about the traps of a radical emancipatory process. Lacan offers an exemplary case in this regard. He clearly demonstrated that the basic antagonism of our psychic life is not the one between egotism and altruism but one between the domain of the Good in all its guises and the domain beyond the pleasure-principle in all its guises (the excess of love, of the death-drive, of envy, of duty . . .). In philosophical terms, this antagonism can be best exemplified by the names of Aristotle and Kant: Aristotle's ethics is the ethics of the Good, the ethics of moderation, of the proper measure, directed against excesses, while Kant's ethics is the ethics of unconditional duty, which enjoins us to act beyond all proper measure, even if our acts entail a catastrophe. No wonder many critics find Kant's rigorism too "fanatical," and no wonder Lacan discerned in the Kantian unconditional ethical

---

12 For a detailed analysis of this topic, see Jamadier Esteban Uribe Munoz and Pablo Johnson, "El pasaje al acto de Telémaco: psicoanálisis y política ante el 18 de octubre chileno," to appear in *Política y Sociedad* (Madrid).

command the first formulation of his own ethics of the fidelity to one's desire. Any ethics of the Good is ultimately an ethics of goods— of things that can be divided, distributed, exchanged (for other goods).

This is why Lacan was deeply skeptical about the notion of distributive justice: it remains at the level of the distribution of goods and cannot deal even with a relatively simple paradox of envy—what if I prefer to get less if my neighbor gets even less than me (and this awareness that my neighbor is even more deprived gives me a surplus-enjoyment)? This is why egalitarianism itself should never be accepted at its face value. The notion (and practice) of egalitarian justice, insofar as it is sustained by envy, relies on an inversion of the standard renunciation accomplished to benefit others: "I am ready to renounce it, so that others will (also) *not* (be able to) have it!" Far from being opposed to the spirit of sacrifice, Evil here emerges as the very spirit of sacrifice—a readiness to ignore my own well-being if, through my sacrifice, I can deprive the Other of its enjoyment . . .

This, however, does not work as a general argument against all projects of egalitarian emancipation but only against those which focus on redistribution. One should never forget that distributive justice is a Left liberal (or social-democratic) notion: we remain within the capitalist order of production, as "the only one which really works," and only try to correct the imbalance of wealth by heavily taxing the rich. Our goal today should be more radical. As is becoming more and more clear from the ongoing crises (the Covid-19 pandemic, global warming and forest fires, and so on), the global capitalist order is reaching its limit, threatening to drag the whole of humanity into the abyss of self-destruction. Once we realize this, the cynical liberal conservatism advocated by Jacques-Alain Miller no longer works. Miller endorses the old conservative "wisdom" that, in order to maintain stability, one has to respect and follow routines established by a choice which is always arbitrary and authoritarian. "There is no progressivism which holds," but rather a particular kind of hedonism called "liberalism of enjoyment." One has to maintain intact the routine of the cité, its laws and traditions, and accept that a kind of obscurantism is necessary in order to maintain social order. "There are questions one shouldn't ask. If you turn the social turtle on its back, you will never succeed in turning it back onto its paws."[13]

One cannot but note that Chile in the "permissive" 1990s offers a perfect case of such "liberalism of enjoyment" which maintains intact the routine of the cité. And, indeed, Miller fearlessly spells out the political implications of his notion of the psychoanalyst who "occupies the position of an ironist who takes care not to intervene into the political field. He acts so that semblances remain at their places while making sure that the subjects under his care do not take them as real . . . one should somehow bring oneself to remain taken in by them (fooled by them)."[14] In relation to politics, then, a psychoanalyst doesn't propose projects, he cannot propose them, he can only mock the projects of others, which limits the scope of his statements. The ironist has no great design, he waits for the other to speak first and then brings about his fall as fast as possible . . . Let us say this is political wisdom, nothing more.[15]

This, again, perfectly fits a postmodern society in which those in power have more important things to do than to "propose projects." It is the impotent Left (or extreme Right) which "proposes projects,"

13 Nicolas Fleury, *Le réel insensé: Introduction à la pensée de Jacques-Alain Miller* (Paris: Germina, 2010), p. 96 (quotes in the quote from J.-A. Miller).

14 Op.cit., pp. 93–94.

15 Jacques-Alain Miller, "La psychanalyse, la cité, les communautés," *La cause freudienne* 68 (February 2008), pp. 109–110.

and the cynical psychoanalysts are here to warn against the dangers of such projects . . . But what to do when the turtle (of our social order) *is* already on its back, so wounded that there is no way of turning it back onto its paws? There is no time for warnings against disturbing appearances; appearances are already destroying themselves. Did a self-professed Christian conservative Donald Trump not do more to disturb appearances than all the leftists opposing him? In such moments when social order is in disarray, psychoanalytic theorists tend to promote another type of warning: don't trust the revolutionaries who promise to lead us out of the catastrophe into a new, more just order. This seems to fit well the general psychoanalytic stance according to which even our noblest acts conceal a narcissistic, masochist, libidinal motivation. Jacqueline Rose recalls Freud's fantasy of how tyranny emerged when early humanity was struck by the horror of the Ice Age:[16]

> Man's response to such a brute curtailing of his drives was hysteria: the origins of conversion hysteria in modern times in which the libido is a danger to be subdued. Man also became a tyrant, bestowing on himself unrestrained dominance as a reward for his power to safeguard the lives of the many: "Language was magic to him, his thoughts seemed omnipotent to him, he understood the world according to his ego." I love this. Tyranny is the silent companion of catastrophe, as has been so flagrantly demonstrated in the behaviour of the rulers of several nations across the world today, not least America's soon to be former president, Donald Trump.

Rose draws a general conclusion here: from the Ice Age to today's actual and forthcoming calamities (the pandemic, global warming,

---

16 Jacqueline Rose, "To Die One's Own Death," *London Review of Books* 42, no. 22, November 14, 2020, https://www.lrb.co.uk/the-paper/v42/n22/jacqueline-rose/to -die-one-s-own-death.

nuclear winter after a new global war), the predominant reaction to the catastrophe is the rise of tyranny in one or another form—a global calamity brings out the worst in human nature. She continues:

> Today, in the midst of a pandemic seemingly without end, there are calls for new forms of solidarity in life and in death, and for a new inclusive, political consciousness. How, though, to find a place in this new reality for the darker aspects of being human which, like upside-down sunflowers, remain at the centre of the unfinished project of psychoanalysis? Failing which, with the best will in the world, any move we make in that direction will prove in the long run to be an empty gesture.[17]

While there is a substantial truth in this line of thought, on the other side of the coin, the lesson of psychoanalysis is not just a warning against emancipatory naivety and about deep destructive forces in human nature (i.e., in relation to the transformation of Soviet Communism into Stalinism). The two world wars also mobilized the radical Left and gave birth to revolutions, with the social-democratic welfare state entering its golden age after WWII. Just remember the shock of Churchill losing the UK elections in early 1945 and being replaced by Clement Attlee, a much less charismatic but effective leader of the Labour Party who was, measured by today's standards, very radical. Is Chile not a proof of how a combination of calamities can lead to extraordinary popular mobilization? The pandemic (and the way it was exploited by the state to squash popular protests) was a crucial factor in the rise of APRUEBO. The usual platitude that calamities bring the worst and the best out of us seems closer to truth here.

17 Rose, "To Die One's Own Death."

So what can psychoanalysis tell us about the victory of APRUEBO in Chile? It would be productive to begin with Lacan's notion of the Master-Signifier and apply it to the space of ideology. Let us begin with a comparison between Chile and the United States. One of the bad surprises of the 2020 US presidential elections was how many votes Trump gained outside of what people consider his constituency—among Blacks and Latinos (even poor ones) and many women—plus how many votes Biden gained among old white men who were expected to vote in much larger majority for Trump. This unexpected reversal proves that the Republicans are now, if anything, more of a working-class party than the Democrats, and that the almost symmetric 50/50 division of the US political body does not directly reflect a class division but is the result of a whole series of ideological mystifications and displacements.[18] Democrats are much stronger than Republicans among the new "digital" capitalists (Microsoft, Amazon, and so on), and they are also discreetly supported by the big banks, while many of the impoverished in the poorest parts of the United States support Republican populism. The result is that in November 2020 we can read serious media reports with titles like this: "Can Trump Actually Stage a Coup and Stay in Office for a Second Term?"[19] Before Trump's era, such titles were reserved for reports from so-called rogue states in the Third World; the United States now has the honor of becoming the first First World rogue state.

In stark contrast to this clear 50/50 division, the victorious APRUEBO in the Chilean referendum got no less than 78.27 percent

18 See Mike Davis, "Rio Grande Valley Republicans," in *London Review of Books* 42, no. 22, November 19, 2020, https://www.lrb.co.uk/the-paper/v42/n22/mike-davis/short-cuts.

19 See Sam Levine, "Can Trump Actually Stage a Coup and Stay in Office for a Second Term?", the *Guardian*, November 23, 2020, https://www.theguardian.com/us-news/2020/nov/23/can-trump-actually-stage-a-coup-and-stay-in-office-for-a-second-term.

of the total votes against the "Rejection" option which got only 21.73 percent of the total votes. What is crucial is that this enormous voting gap is directly proportional to the concentration and distribution of wealth and privileges, with a much smaller group of the population being part of the elite (option "Rejection") and a majority group being aware of this social inequality and injustice (option "Approval"). So Chile is unique not because of some exotic particularity but precisely because it renders directly visible the class struggle which is obfuscated and displaced in the United States and elsewhere. Chile's uniqueness (exception) resides in the very universality of its situation.

But here we should avoid the illusion that the disposition of votes in Chile was more "natural," faithfully reflecting the predominant class division, while in the United States the electoral count didn't "reflect" faithfully the class division but was distorted by ideological manipulations. There is nothing "natural" in political and ideological struggle for hegemony—*every* hegemony is the result of a struggle whose outcome is open. The victory of APRUEBO in Chile does not only demonstrate the absence of ideological manipulations, so that the distribution of votes could "faithfully" reflect the class division; APRUEBO won because of a long and active struggle for ideological hegemony.

Here we should use Ernesto Laclau's theory of the struggle for ideological hegemony as, ultimately, the struggle for Master-Signifiers—not only which Master-Signifier will predominate but how this Master-Signifier will organize the entire political space.[20] Let's take an obvious example: ecology, the struggle against global warming and pollution. With the exception of (increasingly rare) deniers, almost everybody agrees that ecological crisis is one of the central issues today, that it poses a threat to our very survival. The struggle turns around what Laclau called a "chain of equivalences": to which other

20 See Ernesto Laclau, *Emancipation(s)* (London: Verso Books, 2007).

signifiers (topics of ideologico-political struggle) will "ecology" be linked? We have state ecology (only a strong state can deal with global warming), capitalist ecology (only market mechanisms can deal with it—higher taxes on products that pollute our environment are the way out), anti-capitalist ecology (the dynamics of capitalist expansion is the main cause of our ruthless exploitation of nature), authoritarian ecology (ordinary people cannot understand the complexity of ecological crisis, we have to trust strong state power supported by science), feminist ecology (the ultimate cause of our troubles is the social power of men who are more aggressive and exploiting), conservative ecology (we need to return to a more balanced, traditional mode of life), etc. The struggle for hegemony is not just the struggle to accept ecology as a serious issue, but much more the struggle for what this word will mean, and how it will be enchained with other notions (science, feminism, capitalism, and so on).

The imposition of a new Master-Signifier is as a rule experienced as "finding the right name" for what we are trying to grasp; however, this act of "finding" is productive—it establishes a new symbolic field. In Chile, the Master-Signifier of the ongoing protests and of the APRUEBO movement is "dignity." And Chile is not an exception here: in spite of poverty, hunger, and violence, in spite of economic exploitation, the protests that are erupting from Turkey and Belarus to France regularly evoke dignity. Again, there is nothing specifically leftist or even emancipatory in "dignity." If one were to ask Pinochet himself about it, he would without any doubt celebrate dignity, although as included in a different "chain of equivalences" along the patriotic-military line that his 1793 coup saved Chile's dignity from a totalitarian leftist threat. For the partisans of APRUEBO, on the contrary, "dignity" is linked to social justice that will diminish poverty, universal health care, guaranteed personal and social freedoms, etc. It is the same with "justice." Pinochet would undoubtedly advocate justice, but his kind of justice, not the egalitarian economic justice—"justice" would here mean that everybody, especially those at the bottom, should know their proper place. One of the reasons for the triumph of APRUEBO was that they won the struggle for hegemony, so that if now "dignity" and "justice" are mentioned in Chile, they mean what APRUEBO stands for.

This, of course, doesn't imply that political or economic struggles can be reduced to discursive conflicts. What it does imply is that the level of discourse has its own autonomous logic, not only in the sense that economic interests cannot be directly translated into symbolic space but in the more radical sense that how economic and social interests are perceived is already mediated by discursive processes. A simple example: when a country is starving, hunger is a fact—but what matters is how this fact is experienced. Is its cause attributed to Jewish financiers, or is it perceived as a fact of nature (bad weather) or as an effect of class exploitation? Another example: only after the rise of feminism was the subordinated role of women in their families and their exclusion from social life perceived as an injustice; before that moment, to be married to a loving husband and well provided for was considered great luck. The first step of feminism is not a direct step toward justice but the awareness of women that their situation is unjust. In a homologous way, workers don't protest when they live in poverty; they protest when they experience their poverty as an injustice for which the ruling class as well as the state are responsible.

Those who are ready to dismiss these considerations as a step toward "discursive idealism" should remember how Lenin was obsessed with details in political programs, emphasizing how "every little difference may become a big one if it is insisted on,"[21] and how one word (or its absence) in a program can change the destiny of a

---

21 V.I. Lenin, *One Step Forward, Two Steps Back,* available at https://www.marxists.org/archive/lenin/works/1904/onestep/.

revolution. These words are not big central programmatic ideas, they depend on a concrete situation:

> Every question "runs in a vicious circle" because political life as a whole is an endless chain consisting of an infinite number of links. The whole art of politics lies in finding and taking as firm a grip as we can of the link that is least likely to be struck from our hands, the one that is most important at the given moment, the one that most of all guarantees its possessor the possession of the whole chain.[22]

Remember that in 1917, Lenin's slogan for the revolution was not "socialist revolution" but "land and peace," the desire of broad masses to own the land they were working on and to see the end of the war. History is not an objective development but a dialectical process in which what "really goes on" is inextricably mediated by its ideological symbolization. This is why, as Walter Benjamin repeatedly pointed out, history changes the past, i.e., it changes how this past is present today, as part of our historical memory.[23] Let's imagine that Pinochet's re-normalization were to remain and that the protests that began in October 2019 were quickly suppressed; let's further imagine that in this process of false normalization, the figure of Pinochet himself was discarded and his coup condemned. Such a gesture of settling accounts with the Pinochet of the past would have meant the ultimate triumph of the legacy of Pinochet: this legacy would survive in the constitution that grounds the existing social order, his dictatorship would be reduced to a short violent interruption between two periods of democratic normality . . . But this didn't happen, and what took place

22 V.I. Lenin, *What Is To Be Done?*, available at https://www.marxists.org/archive/lenin/works/1901/witbd/v.htm.

23 See Walter Benjamin, "Theses on the Philosophy of History," in *Illuminations* (New York: Mariner Books, 2019).

in Chile in 2019–2020 changed history; a new narrative of the past imposed itself, a narrative which "de-normalized" the post-Pinochet democracy as a continuation of his rule with democratic means.

"Toward a new signifier" is the expression Lacan used in a seminar that took place on March 15, 1977, in the years after he dissolved his school, admitting its (and his own) failure.[24] At the level of theory, this search for a new signifier indicates that he desperately tried to move beyond the central topic of his teaching in the 1960s: the obsession with the Real, a traumatic/impossible core of jouissance that eludes every symbolization and can only be briefly confronted in an authentic act of blinding force. Lacan is no longer satisfied with such an encounter of a central gap or impossibility as the ultimate human experience; he sees the true task in the move that should follow such an experience, the invention of a new Master-Signifier which will locate the gap/impossibility in a new way. In politics, this means that one should leave behind the false poetry of great revolts which dissolve the hegemonic order. The true task is to impose a new order, and this process begins with new signifiers. Without new signifiers, there is no real social change.

---

24 See Jacques Lacan, "Vers un signifiant nouveau," Séminaire du 15.03.77, in *Ornicar?* 17/18.

7.

LEFT LABOUR'S LOSS: A POST-MORTEM

The UK Labour Party lost the 2019 general election for a bunch of reasons—here are three of my own.

Since, in some sense, the elections were about Brexit, the first thing that strikes the eye is the asymmetry in the position of the two big parties: the Tories repeated their chant "Get Brexit done!" while Labour's stance was the worst possible. Knowing full well that its voters were almost symmetrically split into remainers and leavers, Labour was afraid to choose one side and thus lose voters opposed to it—but, as the saying goes, if you try to sit on two chairs simultaneously you may well fall into the gap that separates them. What made things worse was that the true stance of Corbyn was more or less known: he wanted a Brexit, just a different one. He wanted the United Kingdom to be free of the financial and other regulations of the European Union in order to pursue more radical leftist changes. Whatever we think of this choice—there are good reasons for and against Brexit—the Labour Party avoided an open debate about it and masked its indecision with a catastrophic formula: "We'll let the people decide!" Why catastrophic? Because people don't want politicians to impose hard decisions on them; they expect political leaders to show them a clear path, to tell them what choice to make. The Tories clearly did this.

The second reason was the well-orchestrated campaign of character assassination against Corbyn, who was even announced as the

"Top Anti-Semite" of 2019 by the Simon Wiesenthal Center (ahead of actual terrorists!) just days ahead of the general election[25]—a case of foreign meddling at least as strong as the alleged Russian meddling into the 2016 US elections. Gideon Levy correctly predicts[26] that the precipitous conflation of the critique of Israeli politics with anti-Semitism will give rise to a new wave of anti-Semitism, and one can clearly see where this conflation will eventually end. As Marxism taught us, anti-Semitism is a displaced anti-capitalism; it projects the cause of social antagonisms engendered by capitalism onto an external intruder (the "Jews"). The temptation here is to take a fateful step further and to denounce any radical anti-capitalism as a form of anti-Semitism, and signs of this are already multiplying all around the world. Can one imagine a more dangerous way of inciting anti-Semitism?

Last but not least, the third reason for the Labour Left's loss is what I call the Piketty trap. In his *Capital and Ideology*, Thomas Piketty proposes a set of radical measures, and he is fully aware that the model he proposes would only work if enforced globally, beyond the confines of nation-states. As such, it presupposes an already existing global power with the strength and authority to enforce it. However, such a global power is unimaginable within the confines of today's global capitalism and the political mechanisms it implies. In short, if such a power were to exist, *the basic problem would already have been resolved.* Piketty's proposal is utopian, although he presents it as pragmatic, looking for a solution within the frame of capitalism and democratic procedures. If Corbyn had won (or, for that matter, Bernie Sanders

---

25 Hana Levi Julian, "Jeremy Corbyn Rated Top Anti-Semite of 2019 By Simon Wiesenthal Center," *Jewish Press*, December 8, 2019, https://www.jewishpress.com/news/jewish-news/antisemitism-news/jeremy-corbyn-rated-top-anti-semite-of-2019-by-simon-wiesenthal-center/2019/12/08/.

26 Gideon Levy, "From Now On, Every Palestinian Is an Anti-Semite," Haaretz, December 8, 2019, https://www.haaretz.com/world-news/europe/.premium-from-now-on-every-palestinian-is-an-anti-semite-1.8230347.

became US president), just imagine the shattering counter-attack by big capital, with all its dirty tricks . . . Maybe voters were aware of these potential dangers of a Labour victory and preferred to play the safe game.

The challenges that we face, from global warming to refugees, digital control, and biogenetic manipulations, require nothing less than a global reorganization of our societies. Whichever way this happens, two things are sure: it will not be enacted by some new version of a Leninist communist party, but it will also not happen as part of our parliamentary democracy. It will not be just a political party winning more votes and enacting social democratic measures.

This brings us to the fatal limitation of democratic socialists. Back in 1985, Felix Guattari and Toni Negri published a short book in French called *Les nouveaux espaces de liberte*, whose title was changed for the English translation into *Communists Like Us*. The implicit message of this change was the same as that of democratic socialists: "Don't be afraid, we are ordinary guys like you, we don't pose any threat; when we win, life will just go on as usual . . ." This, unfortunately, is not an option. Radical changes are needed for our survival, and life will *not* go on as usual; we will have to change even in our innermost feelings and stances.

This is not to say that we shouldn't of course fully support Labour in the United Kingdom, democratic socialists in the United States, and so on. If we just wait for the right moment to enact a radical change, it will never arrive; we have to begin with where we are. But we should do this without illusions, fully aware that our future will demand much more than electoral games and social democratic measures. We are at the beginning of a dangerous voyage on which our survival depends.

8.

YES, ANTI-SEMITISM IS ALIVE AND WELL—BUT WHERE?

We are now in the midst of a global Zionist offensive whose victims include many Jews who are critical of Israeli politics. One of these is the so-called "propagandist for Hamas," Gideon Levy, who wrote in *Haaretz* on December 8:

> Laws labeling anti-Zionism as anti-Semitism and the anti-occupation movement as anti-Semitic, are passed with over-whelming majorities. Now they are playing into the hands of Israel and the Jewish establishment, but they are liable to ignite anti-Semitism when questions arise about the extent of their meddling.[27]

I consider Levy a true "patriotic Israeli," as he once designated himself. He correctly predicts that the precipitous conflation of the critique of Israeli politics with anti-Semitism will give rise to a new wave of anti-Semitism—how? In order to ground its Zionist politics, the state of Israel is making a catastrophic mistake: it has decided to downplay the so-called "old" (traditional European) anti-Semitism, focusing instead on the "new" and allegedly "progressive" anti-Semitism which it claims is masked in the critique of Zionism. Along these lines,

---

27 Levy, "From Now On, Every Palestinian Is an Anti-Semite."

Bernard Henri-Levy (in his 2008 *The Left in Dark Times*) claimed that the anti-Semitism of the twenty-first century will be "progressive" or there will be none. Brought to its end, this thesis compels us to turn around the old Marxist interpretation of anti-Semitism as a mystified or displaced anti-capitalism (where instead of blaming the capitalist system, our rage is focused on a specific ethnic group accused of corrupting the system). For Henri-Levy and his partisans, today's anti-capitalism is a disguised form of anti-Semitism.

What I find especially worrying is the way that Christian conservatives in the United States combine a strong pro-capitalist stance with a newly discovered love for Israel. How can these Christian fundamentalists, who are as it were by nature anti-Semitic, now passionately support the Zionist policy of the state of Israel? There is only one answer to this enigma: it is not that the Christian fundamentalists have changed, it is that Zionism itself, in its hatred of Jews who do not fully identify with the politics of the state of Israel, has paradoxically become anti-Semitic. This is what Rudy Giuliani recently said against George Soros:

> Don't tell me I'm anti-Semitic if I oppose him. Soros is hardly a Jew. I'm more of a Jew than Soros is. I probably know more about—he doesn't go to church, he doesn't go to . . . synagogue. He doesn't belong to a synagogue, he doesn't support Israel, he's an enemy of Israel. He's elected eight anarchist DAs in the United States. He's a horrible human being.[28]

In a similar display of latent anti-Semitism sustaining a pro-Zionist stance, Trump, speaking before the Israeli American Council in December 2019, used anti-Semitic stereotypes to characterize Jews as driven by money and insufficiently loyal to Israel. The title of the *Vanity*

---

28 Olivia Nuzzi, "A Conversation with Rudy Giuliani Over Bloody Marys at the Mark Hotel," *New York Intelligencer*, December 23, 2019, http://nymag.com/intelligencer/2019/12/a-conversation-with-rudy-giuliani-over-bloody-marys.html.

Fair report on the occasion tells it all: "Trump Goes Full Anti-Semite in Room Full of Jewish People." According to the report, Trump

> started off by once again invoking the age-old cliché about "dual loyalty," saying there are Jews who "don't love Israel enough." After that warm-up he dove right into the stereo-type about Jews and money, telling the group: "A lot of you are in the real estate business, because I know you very well. You're brutal killers, not nice people at all," he said. "But you have to vote for me—you have no choice. You're not gonna vote for Pocahontas, I can tell you that. You're not gonna vote for the wealth tax. Yeah, let's take 100 percent of your wealth away!" He continued: "Some of you don't like me. Some of you I don't like at all, actually. And you're going to be my biggest supporters because you're going to be out of business in about 15 minutes if they get it. So I don't have to spend a lot of time on that.[29]

One almost feels an uneasy embarrassment when confronted with such statements. There is no need for a complex "critique of ideology" here; what should have been just implied is openly spelled out. The line of thought could not be clearer: you are Jews and, as such, you only care about money, and you care about your money more than about your country, so you don't like me and I don't like you, but you will have to vote for me if you want to protect your money . . . The enigma is: why do many Zionists nonetheless respond positively to Trump's message? Again, there is only one consistent answer: because Zionism itself is in some sense anti-Semitic.

---

29 Bess Levin, "Trump Goes Full Anti-Semite in Room Full of Jewish People," *Vanity Fair*, December 9, 2019, https://www.vanityfair.com/news/2019/12/donald-trump-anti-semitic-remarks.

Israel is here playing a dangerous game. Some time ago, Fox News, the main voice of the US radical Right and a staunch supporter of Israeli expansionism, had to demote its most popular host, Glen Beck, whose comments were becoming openly anti-Semitic. When Trump signed the controversial executive order on anti-Semitism at the White House Hanukkah party in 2019, in attendance was John Hagee, the founder and National Chairman of the Christian Zionist organization Christians United for Israel. On the top of the standard Christian-conservative agenda (Hagee sees the Kyoto Protocol as a conspiracy aimed at manipulating the US economy; in his bestselling novel *Jerusalem Countdown*, the antichrist is the head of the European Union), Hagee has made statements that are definitely anti-Semitic: he has blamed the Holocaust on Jews themselves; he has stated that Hitler's persecution was a "divine plan" to lead Jews to form the modern state of Israel; he calls liberal Jews "poisoned" and "spiritually blind"; he admits that the preemptive nuclear attack on Iran that he favors will lead to the deaths of most Jews in Israel. (As a curiosity, he claims in *Jerusalem Countdown* that Hitler was born from a lineage of "accursed, genocidally murderous half-breed Jews.") With friends like these, Israel really doesn't need enemies.

While the struggle between hardline Zionists and Jews open to a true dialogue with Palestinians is crucial, we should not forget the background of this struggle: the West Bank Palestinians, exposed to daily administrative and physical terror (crops burned, wells poisoned), and manipulated by Arab regimes all around them . . . While the true conflict is not the one between "Jews" and "Arabs," it is also not a kind of collective psycho-drama of divided Jews in which Palestinians are just a background voice. There is no way out without an authentic Palestinian voice.

9.

A PERFECTLY RATIONAL ACT . . .
IN A MAD WORLD

The predominant liberal reaction to the US killing of General Soleimani in January 2020 is that it was an act of madness, a reckless display of brutal power with no consideration of long-term effects, so that now all forces of reason and moderation should work together to prevent a catastrophe . . . In short, the motto is: no war with Iran!

But what if the killing was an act that in some sense fitted both sides and was thus perfectly rational from their respective standpoints? What if the United States, the Saudis, and Israel want to push Iran into a massive act of revenge that would finally appear to justify a full strike against the country and thus prevent it from acquiring a nuclear bomb as well as eliminate it as a serious factor in the Middle East? As for Iran, one should just recall the news from the prior two months, now eclipsed by the new tension with the United States: massive demonstrations triggered by the rise of gasoline prices, which have given voice to a large-scale dissatisfaction that included the poor who were otherwise supportive of the regime. This led to the deadliest political unrest since the Islamic Revolution forty years ago, with at least 180 people killed—and possibly hundreds more—as angry protests were smothered in a government crackdown of unbridled force.[30] Many

---

30 Farnaz Fassihi and Rick Gladstone, "With Brutal Crackdown, Iran Is Convulsed by Worst Unrest in 40 Years," *New York Times*, December 3, 2019, https://www .nytimes.com/2019/12/01/world/middleeast/iran-protests-deaths.html.

have compared the recent killing spree to the infamous 1978 Black Friday massacre on Jaleh Square in Tehran, which led to the downfall of Shah Mohammed Reza Pahlavi a year later at the hands of the Islamic revolutionaries who now rule the country, so that the circle is now closed . . . With the new international tension, the ruling elite, which was losing its legitimacy due to rising economic woes, is now again able to mobilize crowds for massive displays of patriotic fervor.

How did we arrive at this point? Retrospection is needed: old debts are collected today; past sins from which the present mess has arisen continue to haunt us. The original sin occurred in 1953 when the CIA organized a coup in Iran to overthrow the moderately progressive regime of President Mosaddegh. This was perhaps the first postmodern coup, staged as a popular carnival, and the CIA even hired the two biggest gangsters of the South Tehran ghetto to mobilize people in protest against Mosaddegh. With this coup, the Shah was able to impose his authoritarian secular modernization, opening up the space for the Muslim clerics to organize popular dissatisfaction.

Then the focus shifted to Iraq, where the United States played a dangerous double game. It first discreetly supported Saddam Hussein in his aggression on Iran soon after the Khomeini revolution, when Saddam thought he could exploit the chaos in Iran to grab its rich oil fields in the south-west. Then, after this strategy miserably failed and Saddam turned his eyes on Kuwait, the US attacked and occupied Iraq itself without a precise feasible plan for what to do there afterward. So the main result of the US's "liberation" of the country is that, instead of serving as a bulwark against Iran, Iraq is now politically under Iranian domination.

The third stage began with the rise of ISIS. Since Shias were targeted by the Sunni ISIS, and since for Israel the Shia Iran was the main threat, Israel discretely supported (or "tolerated") ISIS against Hezbollah in southern Lebanon and Syria. Turkey also played this game. Had Turkey placed the same kind of absolute blockade on ISIS territories as it has on Kurdish-held parts of Syria, let alone shown the same sort of "benign neglect" toward the armed Kurds that it has shown to ISIS, ISIS would have collapsed much faster. Similarly, Saudi Arabia silently welcomed the ISIS war on Shia Islam. This allowed Iran to step in as the savior of Iraq from ISIS when ISIS was already close to Baghdad (the defense was organized by Soleimani himself). This is the price one pays when one's allies are countries like Saudi Arabia and Turkey.

When placed in historical context, the killing of Soleimani can thus be grasped not as an act of madness but as a perfectly rational act in a world that has gone mad. It is this basic madness that we should address, instead of squabbling about secondary control measures that may just pour more oil on the fire.

10.

WINNERS AND LOSERS OF THE IRANIAN CRISIS

One of my favorite kinds of jokes are the American medical ones that follow the formula "first the bad news, then the good news . . ." Here is a slightly tasteless one: after his wife has undergone a long and risky operation, the husband approaches the doctor and inquires about the outcome. The doctor begins: "Your wife survived; she will probably live longer than you. But there are some complications: she will no longer be able to control her anal muscles, so shit will drip continuously out of her anus. There will also be a continuous flow of a bad-smelling yellow jelly from her vagina, so any sex is out. Plus her mouth will malfunction and food will be falling out of it . . ." Noticing the expression of panic gradually appearing on the husband's face, the doctor pats him amiably on the shoulder and smiles: "Don't worry, I was just joking! Everything is OK—she died during the operation."

My good friend Kamran Baradaran wrote me to say that this joke provides a very good description of the present situation in Iran, which narrowly avoided all-out war with the United States after the latter assassinated Iranian major general Qasem Soleimani in a drone strike. First there was a succession of bad news that qualified the successful operation (the killing of Soleimani): skepticism from US allies about the act, furious crowds in anti-American protests, and threats of Iranian revenge that could trigger a large-scale war . . . Then a (fragile and temporary) balance was restored, but this apparent resolution resembles the punchline of our joke: "Don't worry, the crisis was just a joke! Everything is OK," except that nothing is resolved, and the mortifying geopolitical games that place us in permanent crisis are resumed.

It looked as if the killing of Soleimani served both sides. In Iran it led to a popular mobilization and a triumphant display of unity that momentarily obliterated internal struggles; for the US it seemed to open a path toward a war that would eliminate the Iranian threat. Now we see that nobody really wanted a war.

What is the situation in Iran now? The shooting-down of the Ukraine International Airlines plane in January 2020 sparked a resurgence of popular unrest that now threatens the very foundations of the Khomeini revolution—its basic legitimacy, not just the hard-liners' predominance, is openly questioned. The regime's attempt to use the tension with the United States as a means to mobilize the population in its support has backfired, and the regime is more in peril than ever. The unforeseeable shooting-down of the Ukrainian plane thus only served Trump's strategy: Trump doesn't have to start a war against Iran since it looks like Iran is drowning in its own problems.

The reality, however, is that whatever the final result of the Iranian crisis, the United States is not only rapidly losing its grip on Iraq but is also being gradually pushed out of much of the Middle East. The fake "solution" of the crisis with the Kurds in Syria—Turkey and Russia imposing peace so that each one controls its own side—is now being repeated in Libya, and in both cases the United States silently withdrew from playing an active role. Russia and Turkey are now in an ideal position to exert pressure on Europe: the two countries control the oil supply to Europe, as well as the flow of refugees, and can use both as a means of blackmail.

But what if Trump wants this? There are ominous signs that point to YES. Trump is now threatening to move the customs war from China to the EU, and it is clear that the hatred of a strong EU is what unites Trump, Russia, and Turkey. And which Europe is it that bothers Trump, Putin, and Erdoğan, and other European populists? It is the Europe of transnational unity, the Europe vaguely aware that, in order to cope with the challenges of our moment, we should move beyond the constraints of nation-states; the Europe that also desperately strives to somehow remain faithful to the old Enlightenment motto of solidarity with victims; the Europe aware of the fact that humanity is today One, that we are all on the same "Spaceship Earth," and that others' misery is our own problem too. Europe lies in the great pincers between America on the one side and Russia on the other, both of whom want to dismember it—both Trump and Putin support Brexit and euro-sceptics in every corner, from Poland to Italy.

The big loser of the ongoing Middle East crisis is thus Europe, much more than the United States.

11.

HAS AMERICA REALLY LOST ITS MORAL LEADERSHIP?: HOW THE UNITED STATES IS BECOMING A FOUR-PARTY SYSTEM

In February 2020, while promoting his new film in Mexico City, Harrison Ford said that "America has lost its moral leadership and credibility."[31] Really? When did the United States exert moral leadership over the world? Under Reagan or Bush? They lost what they never had, which is to say that they lost the illusion ("credibility" of the claim) of having moral leadership. The Trump era only made visible what was always already true. Back in 1948, at the outset of the Cold War, this truth was formulated with brutal candor by George Kennan:

> We [the US] have 50 per cent of the world's wealth but only 6.3 per cent of its population. In this situation, our real job in the coming period . . . is to maintain this position of disparity. To do so, we have to dispense with all sentimentality . . . we should cease thinking about human rights, the raising of living standards and democratisation.[32]

31 Ed Mazza, "Harrison Ford: America Has Lost Its Moral Leadership and Credibility," HuffPost, February 6, 2020, https://www.yahoo.com/huffpost/harrison-ford-us-leadership-095232005.html.

32 George Kennan in 1948, *quoted in* John Pilger, *The New Rulers Of the World* (London: Verso Books, 2002), p. 98.

Here we find what Trump means by "America first!" in much clearer and more honest terms. So we should not be shocked when we read that "the Trump administration, which came into office pledging to end 'endless wars,' has now embraced weapons prohibited by more than 160 countries, and is readying them for future use. Cluster bombs and anti-personnel land mines, deadly explosives known for maiming and killing civilians long after the fighting ended, have become integral to the Pentagon's future war plans."[33]

But those who deplore the loss of American moral leadership do not care about such facts. What they are preoccupied with is Trump's style. Trump exemplifies the new figure of an openly obscene political master in disdain of the basic rules of decency and democratic openness. Pete Wehner, who held a senior White House post under President George W. Bush, recently said: "We've had presidents who were more moral, or less moral. We've never had a president who takes psychic delight in shattering moral norms, or discrediting morality as a concept."[34] The logic that underlies Trump's actions was spelled out by Alan Dershowitz (among other things, an advocate of legalized torture) who in January 2020

> claimed on the Senate floor that if a politician thinks his re-election is in the national interest, any actions he takes towards that end cannot by definition be impeachable. "And if a president did something that he believes will help him get

---

33 John Ismay and Thomas Gibbons-Neff, "160 Nations Ban These Weapons. The US Now Embraces Them," the *New York Times*, February 6, 2020, https://www.chicagotribune.com/nation-world/ct-nw-nyt-land-mines-cluster-bombs-20200209-iljfzz33zndsda5cbo2tqnlfmq-story.html.

34 John Harwood, "Trump's Historical Place Defined By His Amorality," CNN, February 12, 2020, https://edition.cnn.com/2020/02/12/politics/amorality-presidency-donald-trump/index.html.

elected, in the public interest, that cannot be the kind of quid pro quo that results in impeachment."[35]

The nature of power existing outside of any serious democratic control is here clearly spelled out.

But what about the classic argument for appearances? Namely that, even if we only hypocritically pretend to be moral, appearance nonetheless has an actuality of its own—it compels us to act in a certain way that is better than direct shameless obscenity. Pretending to be moral may seduce us into effectively being a little bit more moral, or, as they say in Alcoholics Anonymous, "Fake it till you make it." The gap between appearance and reality also enables one to take a critical stance toward reality. To the extent that the Marxist critique of "formal freedom" is based on the insight that a "bourgeois" society isn't faithful to its own precepts of freedom and equality, such a critique also takes the ruling ideology more seriously than it takes itself . . . The problem is that, once we enter the domain of pure cynical obscenity, such an immanent critical strategy loses its ground; the return to old decency, hypocritical as it was, is no longer possible, the game is over.

What is discernible in the recent debates about Trump's impeachment is the dissolution of the common ethical substance that makes argumentative polemical dialogue possible. The United States is entering into an ideological civil war within which there is no shared ground to which both parties of the conflict can appeal—the more each side elaborates its position, the more it becomes clear that no dialogue, not even a polemical one, is possible. We shouldn't be too fascinated by the theatrics of impeachment (e.g., Trump refusing Pelosi's handshake, Pelosi tearing up a copy of his State of the Union

35 Stephen Collinson, "Republican Theory for Trump Acquittal Could Unleash Unrestrained Presidential Power," CNN, January 30, 2020, https://edition.cnn.com/2020/01/30/politics/impeachment-analysis-republican-reaction/index.html.

address), for the true conflict is not between the two parties but within each of them.

The United States is transforming itself from a two-party state into a four-party state. There are now really four parties that occupy the political space: establishment Republicans, establishment Democrats, alt-Right populists, and democratic socialists. There are already offers of coalitions across party lines: Joe Biden hinted in late 2019 that he might nominate a moderate Republican as his vice-president, while Steve Bannon mentioned his ideal of a coalition between Trump and Sanders. The big difference is that while Trump's populism easily asserted its hegemony over the Republican establishment, the split within the Democratic Party is getting stronger and stronger—no wonder, since the struggle between the Democratic establishment and the Sanders wing is the only true political struggle going on.

We are thus dealing with two antagonisms: the one between Trump and the liberal establishment (this is what the impeachment was about), and the one between the Sanders wing of the Democratic Party and all the others. The move to impeach Trump was a desperate attempt to regain the moral leadership and credibility of the United States, a comic exercise in hypocrisy. This is why all the moral fervor of the Democratic establishment should not deceive us—Trump's open obscenity just brought out what was always already there. The Sanders camp sees this clearly: there is no way back, US political life has to be radically reinvented.

After enumerating all of Trump's anti-worker and anti-solidarity measures, Julian Zelizer draws attention to how Trump systematically violates the unwritten rules of exerting political power: "All presidents have abided by a certain set of unwritten guidelines when it comes to decorum. The President has thrown all of that out the window. He has normalized a toxic form of presidential speech that undermines our civic culture."[36] Zelizer correctly concludes that while mainstream Democrats are obsessed with the danger of naming a too radical candidate, they miss the key point: "When it comes to public policy and use of political power, no candidate, including Sen. Sanders, would come close to matching the radicalism of the incumbent President." All attempts to "moderate" Trump—including the impeachment hearings—pushed him further to the extreme end of his kind of radicality. The lesson they should adopt is that Trump's radicality is still one that is aimed at protecting the existing system. As the saying goes, Trump is changing some things so that they will basically remain the same. It's too late to return to the old "normal" politeness; the only way to really beat Trump is to do the exact opposite of him and conduct ourselves with decency and good manners, while combining this with radical changes in the content of our acts. It's time for the voice of the true moral majority to be heard.

But is Sanders a true alternative or, as some "radical leftists" claim, is he just a (rather moderate) social democrat who wants to save the system? The answer is that this dilemma is a false one. Democratic socialists in the United States started a mass movement of radical re-awakening, and the fate of such movements is not predestined. Only one thing is sure: the worst imaginable stance is that taken by some Western "radical leftists" who tend to write off the working class in developed countries as a "workers' aristocracy" living off the exploitation of the Third World and caught in racist–chauvinist ideology. In their view, the only radical change can come from the "nomadic proletarian" (immigrants and the Third World poor) as a revolutionary agent (possibly in connection with some impoverished middle-class intellectuals in developed countries). But does this diagnosis hold?

36 Julian Zelizer, "The Most Radical 2020 Candidate," CNN, February 16, 2020, https://edition.cnn.com/2020/02/15/opinions/most-radical-2020-candidate-trump -zelizer/index.html.

True, today's situation is global, but not in this simplistic Maoist sense wherein it is composed of opposing bourgeois nations and proletarian nations. Immigrants are sub-proletarians, their position is very specific; many of them are not exploited in the Marxist sense and are as such not predestined to be the agents of radical change. Consequently, I consider this "radical" choice suicidal for the Left. Instead, I maintain that Sanders is to be unconditionally supported.

The battle will be cruel. Critics of Sanders repeat again and again that he cannot beat Trump on the basis of his all too leftist platform, and that our main focus must be to get rid of Trump. The true message hidden in this argument is: if the choice is between Trump and Sanders, we prefer Trump . . . Even if Sanders were miraculously nominated, and if he (even more miraculously) won the presidency, this would lead to a terrifying counteroffensive. Lloyd Blankfein, former chief executive of Goldman Sachs, said Sanders would "ruin" the US economy.[37] This was not a neutral statement of a fact but expressed a true message of: "I prefer the ruin of our economy to a Sanders victory." But we have no choice here—we have to engage in the struggle with full awareness of the troubled waters that lie ahead.

37 Dominic Rushe, "'This Is What Panic Looks Like': Sanders Team Hits Back After Wall Street Criticism," the *Guardian*, February 13, 2020, https://www.theguardian. com/us-news/2020/feb/13/sanders-campaign-criticizes-panic-from-wall-street-elite -after-new-hampshire-win.

12.

A PLEA FOR A MODERATELY CONSERVATIVE LEFT

With the strikes of French public transport workers dragging on throughout 2020, some commentators have even begun to speculate that France is approaching a kind of revolutionary moment. While we are far from that, what is sure is that the conflict between the state (advocating new unified retirement legislation) and the trade unions (which refuse any changes to what they consider their hard-won rights) leaves no space for compromise.

For a leftist, it is all too easy to sympathize with the striking workers, whom Macron wants to deprive of their hard-won conditions of retirement. However, one should also note that railway and other public transport workers are among those who can still afford to strike. They are permanently employed by the state, and the domain of their work (public transport) gives them a strong position from which to negotiate, which is why they succeeded in getting such a good system of retirement. Their ongoing strike is precisely about retaining this privileged position. There is, of course, nothing wrong with struggling to retain the hard-won elements of the welfare state that today's global capitalism tends to dispense with. The problem is that, from the (no less justified) standpoint of those who do not enjoy this privileged position (precarious workers, youth, the unemployed, etc.), these workers who can afford to go on strike cannot but appear as a class enemy contributing to their own desperate situation—as a new figure of what Lenin called the "workers aristocracy." Those in power can easily manipulate this despair and act as if they are fighting against unfair privileges on behalf of the truly needy workers, inclusive of immigrants.

Furthermore, one should not forget that the public transport workers are addressing their demands to Macron's government, and that Macron stands for the existing economic and political system at its best: he combines pragmatic economic realism with a clear vision of a united Europe, plus he firmly opposes anti-immigrant racism and sexism in all its guises. The protests mark the end of the Macron dream. Recall the enthusiasm about Macron offering new hope not only of defeating the Right populist threat but of providing a new vision of progressive European identity, which brought philosophers as opposed as Habermas and Sloterdijk to support him. Recall how every leftist critique of Macron, every warning about the fatal limitations of his project, was dismissed as "objectively" supporting Marine Le Pen. Today, with the ongoing protests in France, we are brutally confronted with the sad truth of the pro-Macron enthusiasm. Macron may be the best of the existing system, but his politics are located within the liberal-democratic coordinates of the enlightened technocracy.

So what political options are there beyond Macron? There are leftist politicians like Jeremy Corbyn and Bernie Sanders who advocate the necessity of going a decisive step further than Macron, in the direction of changing the basic coordinates of the existing capitalist order while nonetheless remaining within the basic confines of capitalism and parliamentary democracy. They inevitably get caught in a deadlock: radical leftists criticize them for not being really revolutionary, for still clinging to the illusion that radical change is possible through regular parliamentary channels, while moderate centrists like Macron warn them that the measures they advocate are not well thought out and would trigger economic chaos (imagine, if Corbyn had won the 2019 UK elections, the immediate reaction of financial and business circles . . .). In some sense, both critiques are right. The problem is that neither of the positions from which these critiques are formulated work. Ongoing popular dissatisfaction clearly indicates the limits of Macron's politics, while "radical" calls for revolution are simply not strong enough to mobilize the population, often failing to articulate a clear vision of what new order to impose.

So paradoxically the only solution is (for the time being, at least) to engage in the politics of Sanders and Corbyn; they are the only ones who have proven that they can bring about an actual mass movement. We have to work patiently, getting organized so that we are ready to act when a new crisis hits—whether an unexpected ecological catastrophe, or a violent eruption of existing popular dissatisfaction. The radical Left should not seek to get involved in dark plots for how to take power in a moment of crisis (as the Communists were doing in the twentieth century); it should work precisely to prevent panic and confusion when the crisis arrives. One axiom should lead us: the true "utopia" is not the prospect of radical change, but the state of things as they are continuing indefinitely. The true "revolutionary" who undermines the foundations of our societies is not external terrorists or fundamentalists but the dynamics of global capitalism itself.

And the same goes for culture. One often hears that today's cultural war is fought between traditionalists who believe in a firm set of values and postmodern relativists who consider ethical rules, sexual identities, and so on as a result of contingent power games. But is this really the case? The ultimate postmodernists today are conservatives themselves. Once traditional authority loses its substantial power, it is not possible to return to it—all such returns today are a postmodern fake. Does Trump enact traditional values? No, his conservativism is a postmodern performance, a gigantic ego trip. Playing with "traditional values," mixing references to tradition with open obscenities, Trump is the ultimate postmodern president, while Sanders is an old-fashioned moralist.

This is what I mean by a "moderately conservative" Left: a Left that leaves behind the postmodern obsession with marginal transgressions and shamelessly presents itself as the voice of the true moral majority. Today, more than ever, ordinary decent people are not our enemies.

13.

THE AMAZON IS BURNING—SO WHAT?

Just when the burning of the Amazon rainforest had started to disappear from our headlines, in mid-July 2020 we learned that almost four thousand new forest fires were started in Brazil in the two days after the government implemented a ban on the deliberate burning of the Amazon. These figures cannot but trigger alarm. By destroying the Amazon rainforest, we are killing the "lungs of our Earth" and accelerating what appears to be our inexorable march toward collective suicide . . . However, if we want to seriously confront threats to our environment, what we should avoid are precisely such quick extrapolations that fascinate our imagination. Two or three decades ago, everyone in Europe was talking about Waldsterben, the dying of forests. The topic was present on the covers of all the popular weeklies, and there were predictions that in half a century Europe would be without forests. But there are now more forests in Europe than there ever was in the twentieth century, and we are becoming aware of other ecological dangers. While we should take ecological threats extremely seriously, we should also be fully aware of how uncertain analyses and projections are in this domain. We will likely only know for sure what is going on when it is too late. We should avoid making fast extrapolations and contributing to an "ecology of fear," a morbid fascination with looming catastrophe, which only aides global-warming deniers.

An ecology of fear has all the chances of developing into the predominant ideology of global capitalism, a new opiate for the masses replacing the declining role of religion. It takes over religion's fundamental function, that of installing an unquestionable authority which imposes limits. The lesson this ecology is constantly hammering is our finitude, with its message that we are just one species on Earth embedded in a biosphere that vastly transgresses our horizons. In our exploitation of natural resources, we are borrowing from the future. Accordingly, we should treat our Earth with respect, as something ultimately Sacred that should not be unveiled totally—a power we should trust, not dominate. While we cannot gain full mastery over our biosphere, it is unfortunately in our power to derail it, to disturb its balance so that it runs amok, wiping us away in the process. This is why, although ecologists continually demand that we radically change our way of life, underlying this demand is the opposite attitude: a deep distrust of change, development, and progress. This is because every radical change can have the unintended consequence of triggering a catastrophe.

Even when we overcome our fear and profess a readiness to assume responsibility for ecological devastation, this can simply be a tricky stratagem through which we seek to avoid the true dimensions of the threat. There is something deceptively reassuring in readily assuming guilt for threats to our environment. We like to be guilty since, in this case, it all depends on us—if we pull the strings of the catastrophe, then we can save ourselves simply by changing our lives. What is really difficult for us (at least for us in the West) to accept is being reduced to the purely passive role of an impotent observer, who can only sit and watch his fate unfold. To avoid such a situation, we are prone to engage in frantic obsessive activity—recycling old paper, buying organic food, whatever—just to assure ourselves that we are doing something, making our contribution. We are here like the soccer fan who supports his team in front of the TV at home, cheering, booing, and jumping up from his seat in a superstitious belief that this will somehow influence the game's outcome.

It is true that the typical form of fetishist disavowal apropos ecology is: "I know very well (that we are all threatened), but I don't really believe it (so I am not ready to do anything significant in terms of changing my way of life)." But there is also the opposite form of disavowal: "I know very well that I cannot really influence the process which may lead to my ruin, but it is nonetheless too traumatic for me to accept this, so I cannot resist the urge to do something, even if I know it is ultimately meaningless . . ." Is it not for the same reason that we buy organic food? Who really believes that the half-rotten and expensive "organic" apples are really healthier? The point is that, by way of buying them, we do not just buy and consume a product; we simultaneously do something meaningful, show our care and global awareness, participate in a large collective project.

The predominant ecological ideology treats us as *a priori* guilty, as perpetually indebted to Mother Nature. We are under the constant pressure of the ecological superego-agency which addresses us in our individuality: "What did you do today to repay your debt to nature? Did you put your newspaper into the proper recycling bin? And all the bottles of beer or cans of Coke? Did you use your car when you could have used a bike or public transport? Did you use air conditioning instead of just opening the windows?" The ideological stakes of such individualization are easily discernible: I get lost in my own self-examination instead of raising much more pertinent global questions about our entire industrial civilization.

Ecology thus lends itself easily to ideological mystifications: as a pretext for New Age obscurantisms (praising pre-modern "paradigms," etc.); or for neo-colonialism (in the guise of First World complaints about how the rapid development of Third World countries threatens us all); or as a cause of honor for "green capitalists" (buy green, shop local . . . as if taking ecology into account justifies capitalist exploitation). All of these tensions are evident in the predominant reactions to the burning of the Amazon rainforest.

There are five main strategies used to obfuscate the true dimensions of the ecological threat: (1) simple ignorance: it's a marginal phenomenon not worthy of our preoccupation, life goes on, nature will take care of itself; (2) science and technology can save us; (3) leave the solution to the market (higher taxation of the polluters, etc.); (4) emphasis on personal responsibility instead of large systemic measures: each of us should do what we can to recycle, consume less, etc.; (5) advocating for a return to natural balance, to a more modest, traditional life by means of which we renounce human hubris and again become respectful children of our Mother Nature. This last is maybe the worst of them all; the whole paradigm of Mother Nature derailed by our hubris is wrong. The fact that our main sources of energy (oil, coal) are remnants of past catastrophes that occurred prior to the advent of humanity is a clear reminder that Mother Nature is a cold and cruel bitch . . .

This, of course, in no way entails that we should relax and trust in fate. The fact that it is not clear what is going on in our ecological systems makes the situation even more dangerous. What is more, as is fast becoming evident, human migrations are increasingly becoming intertwined with ecological disturbances like global warming. The ecological crisis and the refugee crisis are coming to overlap in the production of what Philip Alston, a UN Special Rapporteur, has aptly called "climate apartheid." In a 2019 report, he said: "'We risk a 'climate apartheid' scenario where the wealthy pay to escape overheating, hunger, and conflict while the rest of the world is left to suffer."[38] Those least responsible for global emissions also have the least capacity to protect themselves.

38 Cited in Damian Carrington, "'Climate Apartheid': UN Expert Says Human Rights May Not Survive," the *Guardian*, June 25, 2019, https://www.theguardian.

So, the Leninist question: what is to be done? There is no simple "democratic" solution to the deep mess we are in. The idea that people themselves should decide (not just governments and corporations) is often put forward, but it begs an important question: even if their comprehension is not distorted by corporate interests, what qualifies them to pass judgment on such a delicate matter? Plus, the radical measures advocated by some ecologists can themselves trigger new catastrophes. Let's take the idea of SRM (solar radiation management): the continuous massive dispersal of aerosols into our atmosphere to reflect and absorb sunlight and thus cool the planet. The risks associated with SRM include decreases in crop yields, irreparable alterations to the water cycle, not to mention the many other "unknown unknowns" that stem from the fact that we cannot imagine how the fragile balance of our earth really functions, and in what unpredictable ways such geoengineering might disturb it.

But what we can do is at least get our priorities straight and admit the absurdity of our geopolitical war games when the very planet for which wars are fought is under threat. The ridiculous game of Europe blaming Brazil and Brazil blaming Europe has to stop. Ecological threats make it clear that the era of sovereign nation-states is approaching its end. A strong global agency is needed with the power to coordinate the necessary measures. And does not the need for such an agency point in the direction of what we once called "Communism"?

com/environment/2019/jun/25/climate-apartheid-united-nations-expert-says
-human-rights-may-not-survive-crisis.

14.

RADICAL CHANGE, NOT SYMPATHY

Pia Klemp, captain of the migrant rescue ship *Iuventa* in the Mediterranean, concluded her explanation for why she decided to refuse the Grand Vermeil medal awarded to her in 2019 by the city of Paris with the slogan: "Documents and housing for all! Freedom of movement and residence!"[39] If the demand here is—to cut a long story short—for every individual to have the right to move to a country of his/her choice, and for this country to have a duty to provide him/her with residence, then we are dealing with an abstract vision in the strict Hegelian sense: a vision that ignores the complex context of social totality. The problem cannot be solved at this level: the only true solution is to change the global economic system that produces immigrants. The task is thus to take a step back from direct criticism to an analysis of the immanent antagonisms of the global situation, with the focus being on how our critical position itself participates in the phenomenon it criticizes.

When conservatives like Margaret Thatcher argue against excessive love for one's neighbor, claiming that this love has to be kept within reasonable limits, they thereby radically change the status of the command "to love thy neighbor." The "impossible" injunction destined to function along the lines of Kant's famous formula, "You

39 "Pia Klemp Refuses the Grand Vermeil Medal Awarded to Her By the City of Paris," Redazione Italia, August 21, 2019, https://www.pressenza.com/2019/08/pia-klemp-refuses-the-grand-vermeil-medal-awarded-to-her-by-the-city-of-paris/.

can because you must!" is turned around into "You must do only what you can, without really disturbing your hard-earned well-being!" and becomes a "realist" strategic consideration. What I am arguing for here is not such a pragmatic "moderation" but, on the contrary, a more radical sharpening of the command. In order to really love one's neighbors in distress, it is not enough to generously give them the crumbs from one's rich table; one should abolish the very circumstances which are causing their distress.

In a recent TV debate,[40] Gregor Gysi, a key figure of the German Linke, gave a good answer to an anti-immigration spokesperson who aggressively insisted that he felt no responsibility for the poverty and horrors in Third World countries and that, instead of spending money to help them, our states should only be responsible for the welfare of their own citizens. The gist of Gysi's answer was: if we don't take responsibility for the Third World poor (and act accordingly), they will come here, to us (which is of course precisely what anti-immigrationists ferociously oppose). Cynical and unethical as this reply may appear, it is much more appropriate than abstract humanitarianism. The humanitarian approach appeals to our generosity and guilt ("We should open our hearts to them, especially given that the ultimate cause of their suffering is European racism and colonization"), and this appeal is often combined with a strange economic reasoning ("Europe needs immigrants in order to continue to expand economically") and a rhetoric around population that is better suited to the Right ("Our birth rates are falling, we are losing our vitality"). The hidden stakes of this operation are clear: let's open ourselves to migrants . . . but only as a desperate measure to avoid the radical change that is actually needed and to maintain our liberal-capitalist order. The logic that sustains Gysi's answer is the opposite: only radical socio-economic change can really protect our identity, our way of life.

40 Accessible at https://www.youtube.com/watch?v=bM0AIh3buig.

The symptom of the prevailing "global leftist" figure is how they simultaneously reject any talk of "our way of life" or of cultural differences, viewing this as a reactionary Huntington stance masking the fundamental identity (or, rather, levelling) of everyone in global capitalism, *and* demand that we respect immigrants' specific cultural identities, i.e., that we don't impose upon them our own cultural standards. The obvious counter-reproach is that "our way" and "their way" of life are not symmetrical since ours is hegemonic. This makes a valid point, but it avoids the core of the problem: the status of universality in the struggle for emancipation. It is true that, in many ways, the refugee is a "neighbor" par excellence, a neighbor in the strict biblical sense: the Other reduced to its naked presence. Without possessions, without home, without a determined place in society, refugees stand for the universality of being human, such that how we relate to them indicates how we relate to humanity as such. They are not just different from us in the sense that all groups of people are different from one another; they are in some sense Difference as such. But, in a properly Hegelian way, universality and particularity coincide here. Refugees come naked only materially, and for this reason they appear to us to cling all the more to their cultural identity. They are perceived as universal, rootless, but at the same time as stuck in their particular identity.

Nomadic immigrants are not proletarians—in spite of the claims of Alain Badiou and others that the "nomadic proletarian" is the exemplary figure of the proletariat today. What makes proletarians proletarian is the fact that they are exploited; they are the key moment of the valorization of capital, their labor creates surplus-value. This is in clear contrast to nomadic refugees who are not only perceived as worthless but are literally "worthless" as the valueless remainder of global capital: the majority of them are *not* included in the process of capital's valorization. Leftists and capitalists alike dream of the new wave of immigrants being integrated into the capitalist machine, as occurred in the 1960s in Germany and then in France, since, they claim, "Europe needs immigrants." Except that this time, it isn't working; immigrants are largely not socially integrated and the bulk of them remain "outside." This fact makes the situation of immigrant refugees much more tragic—they are caught in a kind of social limbo, a deadlock from which fundamentalism offers a false exit. With regard to the circulation of global capital, refugees are put in a position of surplus-humanity, a mirror image of surplus-value, and no humanitarian help and openness can resolve this tension; only a restructuring of the entire international edifice will do.

For Left liberals, the argument for changing the situation in Third World countries in order to abolish the conditions of poverty and war that immigrants flee is often viewed as a (not so) subtle excuse for preventing refugees coming to our countries. The answer to this is clear: in a strictly symmetrical way, "opening our hearts" to refugees is a (not so) subtle way of doing nothing to change the global situation that gives birth to them.

The falsity of humanitarianism is the same falsity found in the rejection of anthropocentrism advocated by deep ecology—there is a deep hypocrisy in it. All the talk about how we, humanity, pose a threat to all life on Earth really just amounts to a concern about our own fate. Earth in itself is indifferent. Even if we destroy all life on Earth, this will just be one—not even the greatest—of the catastrophes that befall it. When we worry about the environment, we worry about our own environment. We want to ensure the quality and security of our lives. The proponents of deep ecology who posit themselves as the representatives of all living beings occupy a position of falsity similar to that of the white anti-Eurocentric liberals who, while ruthlessly rejecting their own cultural identity and soliciting "others" to assert their identities, reserve for themselves the position of universality.

The general lesson to be learned here is that one should avoid at any price cheap humanitarian sentimentalization of those perceived as downtrodden. For this reason alone, *Parasite* (Korea 2019, Bong Joon-ho) is well worth seeing. What the film avoids is any moralizing idealization of the underdogs in the Frank Capra style. We should oppose here content and form: at the level of content, the upper-class Parks are without any doubt morally superior; they are considerate, sympathetic, and helpful, while the underdogs effectively act like parasites, intruding, manipulating, exploiting . . . However, at the level of form, the Parks are the privileged ones who can afford to be caring and helpful, while the underdogs are pushed by their material circumstances into not very gracious acts. The same holds for the common anti-feminist complaint made by men: "I treat women in a kind, unpatronizing way, but they are so aggressive toward me . . ."—of course they are, since for them this is often the only way to counteract their formal submission. As a rule, it is only those at the top who can afford kindness and sympathy.

The solution, then, is not to play the humanitarian game but rather to change the situation that demands humanitarianism in the first place. As Oscar Wilde put it in the opening lines of his "The Soul of Man under Socialism":

> [People] find themselves surrounded by hideous poverty, by hideous ugliness, by hideous starvation. It is inevitable that they should be strongly moved by all this. Accordingly, with admirable, though misdirected intentions, they very seriously and very sentimentally set themselves to the task of remedying the evils that they see. But their remedies do not cure the disease: they merely prolong it. Indeed, their remedies are part of the disease. They try to solve the problem of poverty, for instance, by keeping the poor alive; or, in the case of a

very advanced school, by amusing the poor. But this is not a solution: it is an aggravation of the difficulty. The proper aim is to try and reconstruct society on such a basis that poverty will be impossible. And the altruistic virtues have really prevented the carrying out of this aim.[41]

41 Oscar Wilde, "The Soul of Man under Socialism," (1891), https://www.marxists .org/reference/archive/wilde-oscar/soul-man/.

15.

TRUMP VERSUS RAMMSTEIN

A very strange thing took place recently in the US academic world:

> The Department of Education, in a letter Wednesday, [September 16, 2020] to the president of Princeton University, announced it was investigating the school for lapses in its nondiscriminatory practices . . . The investigation comes after President Christopher L. Eisgruber sent a letter to the school's population about its ongoing efforts to combat systemic racism on September 2. "Racism and the damage it does to people of color nevertheless persist at Princeton as in our society, sometimes by conscious intention but more often through unexamined assumptions and stereotypes, ignorance or insensitivity, and the systemic legacy of past decisions and policies," Eisgruber wrote. The Department of Education's letter cites this phrase as evidence of Princeton's "admitted racism," and is concerned that the school's assurances of nondiscrimination "may have been false" and that the school violated the Title VI of the Civil Rights Act of 1964.[42]

---

42 Elinor Aspegren, "Department of Education Launches Investigation into Princeton University over 'Admitted Racism,'" *USA Today*, September 18, 2020, https://www.yahoo.com/news/department-education-launches-investigation -princeton-005054478.html.

The Department of Education's letter is, of course, ambiguous. If we read it superficially, it is simply yet another super-ego call for a deeper probe into traces of racism, and one can only reproach it for being too radically pedantic. The wording of Eisgruber's letter—racism "nevertheless persists at Princeton as in our society, sometimes by conscious intention but more often through unexamined assumptions and stereotypes"—is part of the standard liberal rhetoric: "the fight against racism is never over, there are always subtle forms of racism that survive," according to which the very claim that there is no racism in our communities is automatically suspicious, itself taken as a sign of racism. The Department of Education's letter takes this purely rhetorical confession literally and demands further action. This is like when an author of a big bestseller admits that their book is by no means perfect, and a journalist then interrogates the author: "If you know it is imperfect, why did you publish it as it is? Why didn't you go on working on it?" But is this literal reading of a rhetorical figure not in itself a sign of something else? Is it not clear that the true reproach to Princeton is not that there is racism in the life of the university but the fact that Eisgruber too openly admitted it? The message to Princeton is thus: practice racism discreetly but don't admit it publicly (in short, the same advice that a Trumpian might discreetly offer to a politically correct liberal).

In another recent example of politically correct regulation, a hate crime bill in Scotland clearly shows its patronizing bias. According to the bill, hate talk in homes, including conversations over the dinner table that incite hatred, must be prosecuted. As reported by the *Times*, justice secretary Humza Yousaf indicated that "Journalists and theatre directors should also face the courts if their work is deemed to deliberately stoke up prejudice."[43] Note not only the implication

---

43 Mark McLaughlin, "Hate Crime Bill: Hate Talk in Homes 'Must Be Prosecuted,'" the *Times*, October 28, 2020, https://www.thetimes.co.uk/article/hate-crime-bill-hate-talk-in-homes-must-be-prosecuted-6bcthrjdc.

that social control should include dinner-table talks, but also the verb "deemed"—the deciding factor is not the intention of the speaker but the perception and opinion of a politically correct observer.

Here is a third similar example: the September 2020 decision by four major art museums in the United Kingdom and United States to postpone for four years "Philip Guston Now," a long-planned retrospective of one of postwar America's most significant artists. In "a cowardly act of censorship," the National Gallery of Art in Washington, D.C., Tate Modern in London, Museum of Fine Arts, Boston, and Museum of Fine Arts, Houston, claimed "that Guston's obviously hostile and darkly satirical images of Ku Klux Klansmen and others could not be exhibited 'until a time at which we think that the powerful message of social and racial justice that is at the center of Philip Guston's work can be more clearly interpreted.'"[44]

This censorship is doubly problematic: it relies on the presupposition that there is an unambiguous single interpretation of a work of art, and, much more problematically, it displays an extremely patronizing stance toward ordinary people. To put it bluntly, the idea is that Guston's work undoubtedly *is* anti-racist and for social justice, but that his "obviously hostile and darkly satirical images of Ku Klux Klansmen" nonetheless could not be exhibited today. Why not? Whom can they still offend even if they are "obviously" anti-racist? I think the answer is multiple. One cannot say that Guston is appropriating Black culture—no, he is "quoting" the worst of *white* culture, and in a way which makes it visible in all its disgusting qualities. The suspicion of a PC viewer is that, even if the truth (of Guston's anti-racism) is obvious, there may be some naïve viewers so fascinated by the imagery mobilized by Guston that they may identify with it,

---

44 Clare Hurley, "Blatant Censorship: Retrospective of American Painter Philip Guston Delayed Four Years, WSWS, October 5, 2020, https://www.wsws.org/en/articles/2020/10/06/gust-o06.html.

missing the satire and critical irony. This is an old procedure also used decades ago by PC liberals in Europe, when the music and accompanying videos (which use "Fascist" military imaginary and sounds) of groups like Rammstein and Laibach was at its peak. Liberals expressed their worries that some naïve ordinary listeners, unaware of the irony and critical distance, would take these bands' performances as directly promoting Fascism. (It didn't matter that all research clearly showed their audiences were almost exclusively leftists, or that, in Germany, Rammstein made clear its preference for *die Linke*, a party to the left of social democracy—the liberal "fear" persisted . . .)

But there is another element at work in the prohibition of Guston's exhibition: a distrust of images as such. Critics behave here like the Freudian unconscious, for which negation doesn't exist. It doesn't really matter how you relate to Guston's images, the very fact of showing them at a deeper level cancels the obvious caricature or critical distance. There is a level at which this holds, of course (in pornography, not to mention snuff movies), but showing it is necessary if we want to effectively undermine the libidinal impact of the depicted phenomenon. Without showing it, one cannot really undermine it from within; one remains at the level of lifeless abstract statements. Therein resides the strength of Rammstein's performances: they stage Fascist rituals in such an exaggerated caricatural way that the ridicule of these rituals becomes palpable. Guston did something similar, but at a different level: he located KKK ideology in the daily misery of its supporters.

Denying the efficiency of critical distance in Guston's work, Kaywin Feldman, director of the National Gallery of Art in Washington, D.C., justified the decision to postpone the exhibition by insisting that we

need to honor the response of viewers and recognize that those are triggering images. Regardless of the artist's intentions, the symbol of the Klansman is a symbol of racial terrorism that has been enacted on the bodies and minds of Black and brown people from our country's founding. The argument of just tell them what to think—it doesn't work when it comes to Klan imagery.[45]

So, again, the idea is that Guston's images of the KKK are "triggering," the verb being the same as in a so-called "trigger warning": "a stated warning that the content of a text, video, etc., may upset or offend some people, especially those who have previously experienced a related trauma."[46]

The obvious point to be made here is: why, then, not add at the entrance to Guston's exhibition such a trigger warning? Feldman's answer would have been that this just amounts to telling the public what to think, which "doesn't work when it comes to Klan imagery." But in this case, this is simply not true. Guston's pictures locate KKK symbols in the repellent misery of the everyday life of a KKK member, depicting what Hegel would have called a *valet de chambre* view of a KKK member (one could well imagine a KKK member protesting at this vulgarization of their noble struggle!); they thus work as a leftist equivalent of a painting which, for instance, depicts in a caricatural way Martin Luther passionately making love to a mistress in a motel room while a bunch of notes for his next speech sits on a nearby table, alcohol spilled on it (as we now know, King did have mistresses). Those "triggered" by such a painting would be followers of King, not his white opponents . . . In both these cases, viewers are

45 Julia Halperin, "Why Did the National Gallery Postpone Its Guston Show?" *Artnet*, October 6, 2020, https://news.artnet.com/art-world/kaywin-feldman-philip -guston-interview-1913483.

46 McKhelyn Jones, "Political Correctness, Trigger Warnings and What to Do about Them," the *Review*, https://www.uvureview.com/news/front-page/recent/opinions/ political-correctness-trigger-warnings.

not asked to think—their reaction of disgust is immediately triggered by the painting itself. This is the key point missed by leftist critics of Rammstein like Thomas Blaser, who writes:

> The German metal band Rammstein's video for "Ausländer" wants it both ways: a critique of colonialism and sex tourism, but right-wing neo-nazis can also enjoy the fascist iconography . . . even though the meaning is ironic. In a mass-consumer democracy, the audience makes their own interpretations. Far Right neo-nazis are reportedly equally attracted to the martial, neo-fascist mise-en-scene as are those who "simply" enjoy the spectacle. Real fascists can ignore the ironic subtlety of the show and lyrics yet indulge in the spectacle that celebrates fascist aesthetics, including black people as happy, naïve savages. In this role as spectators of black ridicule, mainstream audiences join neo-Nazi, alt-Right extremists.[47]

The mistake of this reading is obvious. When Rammstein stages totalitarian rituals, the viewer doesn't need to detect any "ironic subtlety"; these rituals appear strange in their very ridiculous over-presence, in the very disgustingly disturbing excess of enjoyment. And as for the obvious fact that the portrayal of Black people in the "Ausländer" video aligns with white racist clichés—of course, because "Ausländer" is not about real Blacks but about Blacks as part of white racist fantasies. The point is to ruin these fantasies from within, displaying their disgusting ridicule.

There is a fine line of distinction between the distance enacted by bands like Rammstein and the cynical distance practiced by Donald Trump toward extreme Right violent groups. When Rammstein

---

47 Thomas Blaser, "Is Rammstein Racist?" *Africa Is a Country*, July 26, 2019, https://africasacountry.com/2019/07/racism-comes-in-different-guises.

reproduces Nazi rituals, there is no distance; they over-identify with them and in this way subvert them from within. Trump, however, when he is asked about radical rightist groups which propagate violence or conspiracy theories, seeks to formally distance himself from their problematic aspects while praising their general patriotic attitude. This distance is of course empty, a purely rhetorical device. Trump's tacit expectation is that the groups will act upon the implicit calls to violence his speeches are full of. Exemplary here is Trump's answer when asked about the violence propagated and practiced by the Proud Boys. As reported by *Snopes*: "Within minutes after U.S. President Donald Trump told the Proud Boys, a far-right group with members who espouse white supremacism, to 'stand back and stand by,' on national television on Sept. 29, 2020, members of the men-only group took to fringe social media sites to celebrate what they considered a 'historic' moment for their ideological push against leftists."[48] This is (if I may be pardoned for using a problematic expression here) Trump at his best. He does tell the Proud Boys to stand back, i.e., to restrain from violence, but he adds "and stand by," i.e., get ready—to do what? The implication is clear and unambiguous: to violently resist any transition of power to the Democrats.

The paradox is thus clear: Trump's cynical distance toward the white supremacists who support him is much more dangerous than Rammstein's over-identification with Fascism which undermines it from within.

---

48 Jessica Lee, "Who Are the Proud Boys Trump Told To 'Stand Back and Stand By'?" *Snopes*, October 7, 2020, https://www.snopes.com/news/2020/10/.

16.

A DAY OF SHAME INDEED!

On October 29, 2020, Jeremy Corbyn was suspended from the British Labour Party. The decision followed the conclusion of an investigation by the Equality and Human Rights Commission (EHRC), the UK equalities watchdog, into anti-Semitism in the Labour Party, which found that the problem could have been tackled more effectively "if the leadership had chosen to do so."[49] Corbyn was suspended for saying in response to the report that anti-Semitism in the party was "dramatically overstated for political reasons."[50] This act of purge ignited an open conflict between the party's new leader, Keir Starmer, and Corbyn-supporting MPs, among them John McDonnell.

Starmer commented that the EHRC report amounted to "a day of shame" for the party. But what if this was Labour's day of shame for a quite different reason; namely, because Corbyn's suspension took place at all? What if Corbyn was purged not because of his (inexistent) anti-Semitism but because of his critical stance toward capitalism, for which the accusation of anti-Semitism was a cover? Barely a month prior, the Department of Education ordered schools in England not

49 Dan Sabbagh, "Key Findings of the EHRC Inquiry Into Labour Antisemitism," the *Guardian*, October 29, 2020, https://www.theguardian.com/politics/2020/oct/29/key-findings-of-the-ehrc-inquiry-into-labour-antisemitism.

50 See Jessica Elgot and Peter Walker, "Labour Suspends Jeremy Corbyn over EHRC Report Comments," the *Guardian*, October 29, 2020, https://www.theguardian.com/politics/2020/oct/29/labour-suspends-jeremy-corbyn-over-ehrc-report-comments.

to use resources from organizations "which have expressed a desire to end capitalism" because anti-capitalism leads to "opposition to freedom of speech, antisemitism and endorsement of illegal activity."[51] As far as I know, this is the first time such an explicit order prohibiting an anti-capitalist stance has been issued—nothing like this happened even in the darkest times of the Cold War. One should note the words used: "a desire to end capitalism"—not an intention, plan, or program, just a desire, which can of course be projected onto almost any statement ("true, you didn't say it, but you really desire it . . ."). The orders are further highly problematic in their insinuation that a desire to end capitalism is in itself anti-Semitic. The paradox is, of course, that this prohibition is in itself anti-Semitic in its potential implication that Jews are in their essence capitalist. One should note how the standard claim that anti-Semitism is a misplaced anti-capitalism (the Jew is a metaphor for the exploiting capitalist) is here turned around: the secret of capitalism is Jewish domination . . . The sad purge of Corbyn is thus just the latest link in the chain of current anti-leftist propaganda which brands as "anti-Semitic" every agent who takes his critique of the existing order seriously, from Bernie Sanders to Yanis Varoufakis.

Jean-Paul Sartre wrote that if you are attacked for the same text by both sides in a political conflict, this is one of the few reliable signs that you are on the right path. In the last decades, I've been attacked (often on account of the same text!) for anti-Semitism, up to advocating a new holocaust, and for perfidious Zionist propaganda (see Andrew Joyce's November 2019 article in the *Occidental Observer*).[52] So I think I've earned the right to comment on the accusations against

51 Mattha Busby, "Schools in England Told Not to Use Anti-Capitalist Material in Teaching," MSN, September 27, 2020, https://www.msn.com/en-gb/news/uknews/schools-in-england-told-not-to-use-anti-capitalist-material-in-teaching/ar-BB19t30k.

52 Andrew Joyce, "Slavoj Žižek's Pervert's Guide to anti-Semitism," Occidental Observer, November 20, 2019, https://www.theoccidentalobserver.net/2019/11/20/slavoj-zizeks-perverts-guide-to-anti-semitism/.

the Labour Party and Corbyn regarding their alleged tolerance for anti-Semitism.

I, of course, apodictically reject anti-Semitism in all its forms, inclusive of the idea that one can sometimes "understand" it (as in, "Considering what Israel is doing in the West Bank, one shouldn't be surprised if this gives birth to anti-Semitic reactions"). More precisely, I reject the two symmetrical versions of this last argument: "We should understand occasional Palestinian anti-Semitism since Palestinians suffer a lot," as well as "We should understand aggressive Zionism in view of the Holocaust." (One should, too, reject the compromise version: "both sides have a point to make, so let's find a middle way . . .")

Along the same lines, we should supplement the standard Israeli point that the (permissible) critique of Israeli policy can serve as a cover for the (unacceptable) anti-Semitism with its no less pertinent reversal: the accusation of anti-Semitism is often evoked to discredit totally justified critiques of Israeli politics. Where, exactly, does legitimate critique of Israeli policy change into anti-Semitism? More and more, bare sympathy for the Palestinian resistance is condemned as anti-Semitic. Let's take the case of the two-state solution: while decades ago it was the standard international position, given voice in many declarations, now it is increasingly proclaimed to be a threat to the existence of Israel and thus anti-Semitic.

For me, the only way out of this conundrum is the ethical one. There is ultimately no conflict between the struggle against anti-Semitism and the struggle against what the state of Israel is doing in the West Bank. The two struggles are part of one and the same struggle for emancipation. Let's mention a concrete case. In November 2019, Zarah Sultana, a Labour candidate, apologized for a Facebook post in which she backed the Palestinian right to "violent resistance," saying: "I do not support violence and I should not have articulated my anger in the manner I did, for which I apologize."[53] I fully support her apology, we should not play with violence, but I nonetheless feel obliged to add that what Israel is now doing in the West Bank is violence. (Though, certainly, Israel wants peace in the West Bank—occupiers by definition want peace in the occupied land, since it means no resistance . . .) If Jews are in any way threatened in the United Kingdom, I unconditionally and unequivocally condemn it and support all legal measures to combat it—but am I permitted to add that Palestinians in the West Bank face a far greater threat than Jews in the United Kingdom?

Today, the charge of anti-Semitism is more and more levied at anyone who deviates from the acceptable Left liberal establishment toward a more radical leftist stance. Without mentioning Corbyn by name, the UK's chief rabbi Ephraim Mirvis wrote in a November 2019 article for the *Times* that "a new poison—sanctioned from the top—has taken root in the Labour Party."[54] He conceded: "It is not my place to tell any person how they should vote," and went on: "When December 12 arrives, I ask every person to vote with their conscience. Be in no doubt, the very soul of our nation is at stake." I find this procedure of presenting a political choice as a purely moral one ethically disgusting—it reminds me of how, decades ago, the Catholic Church in Italy did not explicitly order citizens to vote Christian Democracy but just said that they should vote for a party which is Christian and democratic . . .

---

53 "Labour Coventry South Candidate Zarah Sultana Apologises For 'Celebrate Deaths' Post," BBC, November 4, 2019, https://www.bbc.co.uk/news/uk-england -coventry-warwickshire-50292235.

54 Ephraim Mirvis, "What Will Become of Jews in Britain if Labour Forms the Next Government?", the *Times*, November 25, 2019, https://www.thetimes.co.uk/ article/ephraim-mirvis-what-will-become-of-jews-in-britain-if-labour-forms-the- next-government-ghpsdbljk.

Slavoj Žižek

A politics of radical choice is, today, the only principled one: we should make a choice where choice is necessary and reject a choice where it is a false one. Today, we should firmly reject the political misuse of Zionism that condemns every sympathy with Palestinians as anti-Semitic, just as we should ruthlessly reject the Islamist terrorism manifested in recent slaughter attacks in Paris and Nice. There is no choice here, no right measure between the two extremes—as Stalin would have put it, they are both worse. That Corbyn took such a principled stance was the true reason for his downfall.

17.

LIMITS OF DEMOCRACY

In the weeks before the 2020 US presidential elections, different forms of populist resistance were forming a unified field, as reported in the *Guardian*:

> Armed militia groups are forging alliances in the final stages of the US presidential election with conspiracy theorists and anti-vaxxers who claim the coronavirus pandemic is a hoax, intensifying concerns that trouble could be brewing ahead of the election day. Leading advocates of anti-government and anti-science propaganda came together at the weekend, joined by the founder of one of the largest militia groups.[55]

Three dimensions are at work here: conspiracy theorists (like QAnon), Covid deniers, and violent militias. These dimensions are often inconsistent and relatively independent: there are conspiracy theorists who don't deny the reality of the pandemic but see in it a (Chinese) plot to destroy the United States; and there are Covid deniers who don't see a conspiracy behind the pandemic but just deny the seriousness of the threat (e.g., Agamben). But the three dimensions are now moving together: violent militias legitimize themselves

---

55 Ed Pilkington, "US Militias Forge Alliances with Conspiracy Theorists Ahead of Election," the *Guardian*, October 14, 2020, https://www.theguardian.com/world/2020/oct/14/armed-militias-conspiracy-theorists-anti-vaxxers-red-pill-expo.

as defenders of freedom which they see as threatened by a deep-state conspiracy against the re-election of Trump, and they see the pandemic as a key element of this conspiracy. In this view, for Trump to lose re-election would be the result of this conspiracy, which means that violent resistance to Trump's loss is legitimate. On October 29, Archbishop Carlo Maria Viganò, a former Vatican ambassador to the United States and outspoken adversary of Pope Francis,

> made waves within the online world of QAnon after his open letter to President Trump was quoted in a post from the anonymous leader of the cult-like conspiracy movement. The letter hit many of the favorite themes of the pro-Trump conspiracy theory, attacking their familiar villains from the ominous "global elite," to Bill Gates and the "mainstream media." "The fate of the whole world is being threatened by a global conspiracy against God and humanity," Viganò wrote, emphasizing the "epochal importance of the imminent election," casting Trump as "the final garrison against the world dictatorship."[56]

The jump to violence is easy from such a standpoint. In October 2020, the FBI revealed that a right-wing militia group planned to kidnap Gov. Gretchen Whitmer of Michigan from her house, taking her to a secure location in Wisconsin where she would undergo a kind of people's "trial" for her "treason."[57] As a governor, she imposed tough restrictions to curb Covid-19 infections and, according to the

56 Caitlin Dickson, "'A Global Conspiracy against God and Humanity': Controversial Catholic Archbishop Pushes QAnon Themes in Letter to Trump," Yahoo, October 31, 2020, https://www.yahoo.com/news/a-global-conspiracy-against-god-and-humanity-controversial-catholic-archbishop-pushes-q-anon-themes-in-letter-to-trump-134003985.html.

57 Derick Hutchinson, "FBI: Group Plotting to Kidnap Michigan Gov. Whitmer Wanted to Take Her to Wisconsin for 'Trial'," ClickOnDetroit, October 8, 2020,

militia group, thereby violated the freedoms guaranteed by the US constitution. Is this plan not reminiscent of the most famous political kidnapping in Europe? In 1978, a key figure of the Italian political establishment who evoked the possibility of the big coalition between the Christian Democrats and the Communist Party was kidnapped by the Red Brigades, put to a trial by a people's court, and shot dead . . .

Angela Nagle was right in arguing that the new populist Right is taking over procedures that were decades ago clearly identified as belonging to extreme Left "terrorist" groups.[58] This, of course, in no way implies that the two "extremes" somehow coincide—we don't have a stable Center symmetrically flanked by the two extremes. The basic antagonism is the one between the establishment and the Left, and the rightist violent "extremism" is a panicky reaction triggered when the Center is threatened. This became clear in the last presidential debate when Trump accused Biden of backing "Medicare for All," saying "Biden agreed with Sanders," to which Biden replied: "I beat Bernie Sanders."[59] The message of this reply was clear: Biden is Trump with a human face—in spite of their opposition they share the same enemy. This is liberal opportunism at its worst: renounce the Left "extremists" out of fear of scaring the center.

And it's not just the United States that is moving in this direction. Let's just take a look at the cover stories in European media: in Poland, liberal public figures complain that they are becoming spectators at the dismantling of democracy; the same in Hungary . . . At an even more general level, a certain tension that is immanent

---

https://www.clickondetroit.com/news/local/2020/10/08/fbi-group-plotting-to
-kidnap-michigan-gov-whitmer-wanted-to-take-her-to-wisconsin-for-trial/.

58 Angela Nagle, *Kill All Normies* (New York: Zero Books, 2017).

59 Peter Sullivan, "Trump, Biden Clash over Health Care as Debate Begins," the *Hill*, 29 September, 2020, https://thehill.com/policy/healthcare/518863-trump-biden -clash-over-lawsuit-against-obamacare-as-debate-begins.

to the very notion of parliamentary democracy is gaining visibility today. Democracy means two things: the "power of the people," or the idea that the substantial will of the majority should express itself in the state; and trust in the electoral mechanism, such that no matter how many manipulations and lies there are, once the numbers are counted the result is to be accepted by all sides. Thus Al Gore conceded defeat to Bush even though more people voted for him and the counting in Florida was very problematic—trust in the formal procedure is what gives parliamentary democracy its stability. Problems arise when these two dimensions get out of sync, and both the Left and the Right often demand that the people's substantial will should prevail over electoral formalities. And in some sense they are right: the mechanism of democratic representation is not really neutral. As Alain Badiou writes, "If democracy is a representation, it first of all represents the general system which sustains its form. In other words, the electoral democracy is only representative insofar as it is first the consensual representation of capitalism, which is today renamed 'market economy.'"[60]

One should take these lines in the strictest formal sense: at the empirical level, of course, the multi-party liberal democracy "represents"—mirrors, registers, measures—the quantitative dispersal of different opinions of the people, what they think about the proposed programs of political parties and about their candidates, and so on. However, prior to this empirical level and in a much more radical sense, the very form of multi-party liberal democracy *"represents"— instantiates—a certain vision of society, politics, and the role of the individuals in it*, whereby politics is organized in parties which compete through elections to exert control over the state legislative and executive apparatus. One should always be aware that this frame is never neutral—it privileges certain values and practices.

60 Alain Badiou, *De quoi Sarkozy est-il le nom?* (Paris: Editions Lignes, 2007), p. 42.

This non-neutrality becomes palpable in moments of crisis or indifference, when we experience the inability of the democratic system to register what people effectively want or think. This inability is signaled by anomalous phenomena like the UK elections of 2005, where, in spite of the growing unpopularity of Tony Blair (he was regularly voted the most unpopular person in the UK), there was no way for this discontent to find a politically effective expression. Something was obviously very wrong here, and it was not that people "did not know what they wanted," but, rather, that cynical resignation prevented them from acting upon it, so that the result was the weird gap between what people thought and how they acted (voted).

A year or so ago, the same gap exploded more brutally with the rise of the *gilets jaunes* (yellow vests) in France. The protests clearly articulated an experience that was impossible to translate or transpose into the terms of the politics of institutional representation, which is why the moment Macron invited their representatives to a dialogue and challenged them to formulate their complaints in a clear political program, their specific experience evaporated. Didn't exactly the same thing happen with Podemos in Spain? The moment they agreed to play party politics and entered government, they became almost indistinguishable from the Socialist Party—yet another sign that representative democracy doesn't fully work.

In short, the crisis of liberal democracy has lasted for more than a decade; the Covid pandemic only made it explode beyond a certain level. The basic premises of a functioning democracy are today more and more undermined. The trust on which democracy relies was best expressed by Lincoln's famous saying: "You can fool all the people some of the time, and some of the people all the time, but you cannot fool all the people all the time." Let's give to this saying a more pessimist spin: only in rare exceptional moments does the majority live in truth; most of the time they live in non-truth while only a minority is aware of truth. The solution is certainly not to be found in some kind of more "true" democracy that is more inclusive of all minorities; the very frame of liberal democracy will have to be left behind, exactly what liberals fear most. The solution is also not that somehow the self-organized and mobilized civil society (e.g., with Podemos, the *gilets jaunes*) directly takes over and replaces the state. Direct rule of the multitude is an illusion; as a rule it has to be sustained in a strong state apparatus. The path to true change opens only when we lose hope in a change within the system. If this appears too "radical," recall that today, our capitalism is already changing, although in the opposite sense.

Direct violence is as a rule not revolutionary but conservative, a reaction to the threat of a more basic change—when a system is in crisis, it begins to break its own rules. Hannah Arendt said that, in general, violent outbreaks are not the cause that change a society but rather the birth pangs of a new society in a society that has already expired due to its own contradictions. Let's remember that Arendt says this in her polemic against Mao, who said that "power grows out of the barrel of a gun"—Arendt qualifies this an "entirely non-Marxist" conviction and claims that, for Marx, violent outbursts are like "the labor pangs that precede, but of course do not cause, the event of organic birth." Basically I agree with her, but I would add that a fully peaceful "democratic" transfer of power cannot happen without the "birth pangs" of violence; there will always be moments of tension when the rules of democratic procedure are suspended.

Today, however, the agent of this tension is the Right, which is why, paradoxically, the task of the Left is now, as Alexandria Ocasio-Cortez pointed out, to save our "bourgeois" democracy when the liberal center is too weak and indecisive to do it. Is this in contradiction with the fact that the Left today should move beyond parliamentary democracy? No. As Trump demonstrates, the contradiction is in this democratic form itself, so that the only way to save what is worth saving in liberal democracy is to move beyond it—and vice versa: when rightist violence is on the rise, the only way to move beyond liberal democracy is to be more faithful to it than the liberal democrats themselves. This is what the successful democratic return to power of Morales's party in Bolivia, one of the few bright spots in our devastated landscape, clearly signals.

18.

THE COURAGE OF COVID HOPELESSNESS

Europe is now paying the price for its summer complacency. First, we thought that the heat of the 2020 summer would kill off the coronavirus pandemic. Then, when the virus did not disappear over summer, we accepted that the heat hadn't worked as expected. Nevertheless, life opened up somewhat, and there was a sense of relief that the worst was over. Now, in the fall of 2020, when the virus is returning with a vengeance, we can see that the summer heat *did* in fact do what it was expected to do: it may not have killed the virus but it clearly did diminish its transmission. Our summer was a brief moment of hope in which we all somehow believed the worst was over. Everywhere one could hear warnings about how we should prepare for the second wave, but these were mostly not acted upon. The logic of fetishist disavowal ("I know very well, but I don't really believe it") again asserted itself with full force, and now we are surprised that what we expected to happen effectively happened. And another excuse is now falling apart: the claim that although infections are sharply rising, death rates remain low, indicating that we are dealing with a much milder mutation of the virus. Covid-19 deaths are clearly on the rise in Europe.

In many European countries that are strongly affected by the pandemic, the state administration is gradually losing control over infections. When, on October 25, 2020, a Trump aide declared, "We're not going to control the pandemic," it caused a scandal.[61] When pressed to explain why the pandemic could not be reined in, White House chief of staff Mark Meadows said: "Because it is a contagious virus just like the flu," explaining that the government was focused on getting effective therapeutics and vaccines to market. This argument is just one in a series of three which cannot but remind us of the famous argument about the broken kettle evoked by Freud: (1) I returned the kettle unbroken to you, (2) the kettle was already broken when you gave it to me, (3) I never even borrowed a kettle from you. The version adopted by Trump's White House is, as Paul Krugman has shown:[62] (1) Covid is a disease that seriously affects only a small number of people, doctors exaggerate it all to get more money; (2) Covid is serious, but we, the administration, are doing a top job; (3) it is an infection that just spreads so there is nothing that really can be done to control it . . .

Many European countries are now doing the same as their health systems approach collapse. Until now, the practice was that if a medical worker came into close contact with an infected person, s/he had to go into quarantine; now, medical workers are obliged to go on working till they show visible signs of illness. Although this measure is justified by the lack of medical personnel, it opens up the way for the virus to spread freely in hospitals, which are already hotspots of infection. And some states (like Belgium and the Czech Republic) have now gone even further, so that even if a medical worker tests positive, s/he is obliged to go on working till the infection gets so strong that s/he approaches collapse. In Berlin, Belgium, the Czech Republic, and Slovenia, those

61 Jonathan Lemire, Alexandra Jaffe, and Aamer Madhani, "Trump Aide: 'We're Not Going to Control the Pandemic,'" AP, October 26 2020, https://apnews.com/article/election-2020-joe-biden-donald-trump-pandemics-virus-outbreak-03de71eecbb9a605 b1efc324cdeb3a5e.

62 See Paul Krugman, "Trump Tells Coronavirus, 'I Surrender,'" the *New York Times*, October 26 2020, https://www.nytimes.com/2020/10/26/opinion/trump -coronavirus-climate-change.html.

experiencing symptoms of Covid-19 were recently told not to even call their doctor unless their situation became very serious. These states also abandoned tracing cases, instructing individuals who developed symptoms to try to remember who they were with and inform them to behave carefully . . . In short, states are capitulating to the virus.

Throughout the last summer, it became popular to argue that lockdowns and quarantines were a medicine worse than the illness itself, that they caused more damage not only economically but even with regard to health (i.e., the knock-on effects of neglecting cancer and other illnesses). The basic axiom was to avoid lockdown at any price. We were repeatedly told that the economy could not afford another halting of social and economic life. But this led to a third wave, to half-baked measures that partially saved the economy but only postponed the resurgence of the virus. Caught between two (or even three) sides—medical experts, business interests, and the pressure of populist Covid deniers—governments adopted a politics of compromises, proposing often inconsistent and ridiculously complex half-measures, for which we are now paying the price in the form of not only a new explosion of Covid-19 infections but also the clear prospect of catastrophic economic hardships. Reality broke through and now European governments are openly considering lockdowns if the trend is not reversed. The problem is that, *within* the socio-economic coordinates of today's global capitalism, they cannot afford another lockdown—it would bring unheard-of economic depression and chaos, social unrest, and mental health crises. One lockdown is all that the global system can take.

Here we are now: the long, hot summer of compromises with the global capitalist order is over, and we are brutally confronted with the limit of state attempts to contain the pandemic without disturbing this order. The situation is hopeless; it is clear that there is no hope of finding a solution *within* the existing order. One has to gather the courage to openly accept this hopelessness and to then propose in its place a radical socio-economic change: a direct "politicization" (socialization) of the economy, with a much stronger role for the state and, simultaneously, much greater transparency of state apparatuses within civil society.

To provide a general sense of the change that is required, let me mention the four components of the idea of revolutionary justice as elaborated by Alain Badiou: voluntarism (the belief that we can "move mountains," ignoring "objective" laws and obstacles); terror (a ruthless will to crush the enemy); egalitarian justice (with no regard for the "complex circumstances" which allegedly compel us to proceed gradually); and, last but not least, trust in the people. The mere mention that this idea might have relevance for our pandemic predicament cannot but trigger horror or laughter—and, above all, claims that we live in a complex postmodern society in which such procedures are not only ethically inacceptable but have been proven inefficient . . . However, the point I wish to make is not only that the ongoing pandemic requires us to invent a new version of these four features, and a much stronger one, but also that we are already doing it. When crisis hit Cuba after the fall of the Soviet Union, the authorities called this new period—characterized by military discipline but without war—"the Special Period in Time of Peace." We all laughed at this name, but do we not now occupy just such a "Special Period in Time of Peace"? Let's go step by step.

Voluntarism. Even in countries where conservative forces are in power, more and more decisions are taken that clearly violate "objective" laws of the market: states directly intervene in industry and agriculture, distributing billions to prevent hunger or implement health care measures. At least a partial socialization of the economy will become even more urgent with the ongoing rise in infections. As in a war, health care will have to be expanded and reorganized without regard for the laws of the market.

Terror. Liberals are correct in their fears: although it is not the old "totalitarian" police terror, serious limitations of our freedoms are now a fact of life. Not only are states forced to enact new modes of social control and regulation, but, in some places, people are being solicited to report to the authorities any family members or neighbors who may be infectious or who break lockdown measures. With the pandemic, whistleblowers are fully established as the new heroic figure. There are of course those who resist the idea that ordinary people should take a role in informing authorities about violations of pandemic rules, seeing this as similar to denouncing one's friends to the police, but we should oppose such false equations.

Egalitarian justice. It is commonly accepted that the eventual vaccine should be accessible to everybody, and that no part of the world population should be sacrificed to the virus—the cure is either global or inefficient. Can it be done? As Immanuel Kant wrote apropos duty: *Du kannst denn du sollst,* you can because you ought to. Of course there will be a lot of cheating going on, but this should be treated as the crime that it is and met with severe punishment. States that try to control the vaccine at the expense of others should be treated as rogue states.

Trust in the people. We all know that most of the measures against the pandemic only work if people follow the recommendations—state control cannot do all the work here. The appeal to compassion is not enough; people should be informed about the dangers and also made adequately scared so that they actually follow regulations. Further, people should be incited to self-organize in local communities to help those in need. And, of course, people should *not* fully trust their state institutions; these institutions themselves should feel the "terrorist" pressure of the people who have the right and duty to treat members of these institutions as suspect.

Resistance to these measures will persist from all sides, but it is just that: resistance against what science is telling us. This is why most of the resistance comes from the populist new Right. There is no space for compromises here. We already spent the precious summer interlude in search of such compromises, and we clearly lost that battle. Now it's time to act ruthlessly. In short, as I claimed months ago, we need in Europe a version of something that cannot but be called "wartime Communism": an all-European state of emergency with strict discipline and the subordination of the economy to coping with all of our ills (not only the pandemic). As for the other ills that are awaiting us, here is a report from our media on October 27, 2020:

> Scientists have found evidence that frozen methane deposits in the Arctic Ocean—known as the "sleeping giants of the carbon cycle"—have started to be released over a large area of the continental slope off the East Siberian coast, the *Guardian* can reveal. High levels of the potent greenhouse gas have been detected down to a depth of 350 metres in the Laptev Sea near Russia, prompting concern among researchers that a new climate feedback loop may have been triggered that could accelerate the pace of global heating.[63]

Does this mean that we should resign ourselves to such a wartime Communism with no end in sight, and forget the social freedoms we are used to? Even if we ignore the fact that these freedoms were actually much more limited than many make out, the paradox is that only by way of passing through the zero-point of "wartime Communism" can we keep the space open for the new freedoms-to-come. If we stick to our old way of life, we will surely end up in a new barbarism. Only if we admit that the situation—if we remain within the existing global order—is hopeless can we find a way out.

63 Jonathan Watts, "Arctic Methane Deposits 'Starting to Release,' Scientists Say," the *Guardian*, October 27, 2020, https://www.theguardian.com/science/2020/oct/27/sleeping-giant-arctic-methane-deposits-starting-to-release-scientists-find.

19.

TRUMP'S BARBER PARADOX

For thirty years, Donald Trump regularly visited the Paul Molé Barber Shop on the Upper East Side of Manhattan. Adrian Wood, the barber who owns the shop, remembers that Trump would instruct barbers precisely where to snip his mane, and would never allow them to expose his bald spot: "He's a complete control freak. He dictates exactly how you cut every hair on his head. 'Cut here, cut there. That's enough.' And you just do what he says."[64] Now, in November 2020, as Trump repeatedly evokes the prospect that before leaving office he might pardon himself amid state investigations into his business and finances,[65] the surrounding debate throws us back into the self-reference paradoxes discussed for millennia—like the one (falsely attributed to Bertrand Russell) about a barber who shaves only those who do not shave themselves. Does this barber shave himself? If he does, then he obviously violates the rule of shaving only those who do not shave themselves. If he doesn't, he falls in the category of those who do not shave themselves, so he can shave himself . . .

64 Sara Dorn, "Donald Trump's Old Barber Says He's a Total 'Control Freak'," *New York Post*, April 7, 2018, https://nypost.com/2018/04/07/donald-trumps-old-barber-says-hes-a-total-control-freak/.

65 Evan Perez, Pamela Brown, Jamie Gangel, and Jeremy Herb, "As Trump Wrestles with Defeat, Pardons Loom For Allies—And Himself," CNN, November 12, 2020, https://edition.cnn.com/2020/11/12/politics/trump-pardons-loom-defeat/index.html.

What happens if we apply this paradox to Trump—can he pardon himself? Common sense tells us that the president (or any other supreme authority like a monarch), who has the right to pardon persons judged and condemned by a court, can only pardon those who cannot pardon themselves (if all condemned could pardon themselves, a large majority of them would do so). If he can pardon himself, then he needs pardon, which means he is a common person who violated the law and, as such, cannot pardon himself . . . But the solution to these paradoxes is, in the case of Trump, relatively simple: Trump himself, the self-professed protector of Law and Order, perceives himself as standing above the Law. The implication of his claim that he can pardon himself is that he ultimately doesn't need to be pardoned because what he does is not contained by the Law.

But there is another problem here: the privilege of giving pardon is usually reserved for monarchs or presidents who do not hold executive power, i.e., whose function is, as we say, symbolic and ceremonial. (Hegel clearly saw the necessity of the gap that separates the monarch from executive power.) "Totalitarian" temptation arises when the two levels collapse into one another, i.e., when the nominal head of state also holds executive power. This happens not only in Fascist and Stalinist "totalitarianism" (although, in the case of Italy, Mussolini did not hold both roles—Italy remained a monarchy) but is also inscribed into the very Constitution of the United States. The United States is unique in that the president is not exempt from executive power, the two functions are united (which is why US presidents can rule with executive orders, largely ignoring Congress and Senate). Where does this prerogative come from? Eric Nelson, in his *The Royalist Revolution*,[66] convincingly demonstrates that it was admiration for royal prerogative power and belief in the virtues of a strong executive, both

66 Eric Nelson, *The Royalist Revolution: Monarchy and the American Founding* (Cambridge, MA: Harvard University Press, 2017).

derived from seventeenth-century precedents, that fostered the rebellion against Britain and shaped the Constitution of the new American republic. The American Revolution came out of a royalist, not a parliamentarian, tradition: first, the Founding Fathers hoped that the British king would protect them against the tyranny of the British parliament raising taxes on the American colonies; when this did not happen, they incorporated this image of a monarch with executive powers into their Constitution.

This decision of the Founding Fathers has fateful consequences even today: what Obama and Trump share, all their contrasts notwithstanding, is the excessive use of executive orders. It is not that the United States is really a monarchy but that, in some sense, it is even worse than a constitutional monarchy; it is like a monarchy in which the monarch also has executive power which can limit parliamentary oligarchy. However, the irony of history teaches us that maybe something good can come out of this danger. Remember how, at the beginning of his presidency, Trump used his executive powers to proclaim a state of national emergency? His critics were shocked at how he applied this measure, clearly intended only for great catastrophes like a threat of war or a natural disaster, in order to build a border wall to protect the United States from an invented threat. However, not only were the Democrats critical of this measure, but some rightists were also alarmed by the fact that Trump's proclamation set a dangerous precedent: what if a future leftist Democratic president proclaimed a national emergency on behalf of, say, global warming? My point is precisely that future leftist presidents should act like this to legitimize fast extraordinary measures—global warming effectively *is* a (not only national) emergency.

20.

HOW TO KILL TRUMP IN HIS NOTION

On November 23, 2020, Donald Trump agreed to begin his transition out of presidential power, but the way his acceptance was announced says a lot about Trump.[67] It followed the General Services Administration's declaration of Joe Biden as the "apparent winner" of the US election, allowing for the formal transition from Trump's administration to begin. Emily Murphy, head of the GSA, stated in a letter to the president-elect that she came to her decision "independently" and did not receive pressure from the executive branch. (Note the reference to Biden as the "apparent" election winner—if the opposite of appearance is essence, this qualification implies that "essentially" Trump won, whatever the final result of recounting!) However, minutes after Murphy's letter was first reported, Trump tweeted that he had given Murphy permission to send the letter, though he vowed to continue protesting his own defeat[68]—his campaign team would continue to push its supporters to back fundraising efforts in a last-ditch bid to beat the election outcome. So Trump accepted the transition

67 See Sam Levin and Maanvi Singh, "Trump Agrees to Begin Transition as Key Agency Calls Biden Apparent Election Winner," the *Guardian*, November 24, 2020, https://www.theguardian.com/us-news/2020/nov/24/trump-transition-biden -general-services-administration.

68 Kevin Breuninger, "Trump Administration Officially Begins Transition to Biden after Weeks of Delay," CNBC, November 23, 2020, https://www.cnbc .com/2020/11/23/trump-appointee-informs-biden-that-gsa-will-begin-transition -process-reports-say.html.

without conceding defeat, permitting acts made independently of his will . . . He is a living contradiction: the ultimate postmodern ironist who presents himself as a guardian of traditional Christian values; the ultimate demolisher of law and order who presents himself as its unconditional safeguard.

A similar tension is found in how Trump relates to the Far Right, and specifically in how he seeks to formally distance himself from its most problematic aspects while praising its general patriotic attitude. This distance is of course empty, a purely rhetorical device. While weakly condemning the worst aspects of groups like the Proud Boys (telling them to "stand back"), Trump simultaneously makes clear his expectation for them to ("stand by" to) act upon the implicit calls to violence in his speeches.

Trump's response to the Proud Boys is just one illustration of how his "excesses" should be taken seriously. In a rare appearance supporting her husband in the 2020 electoral campaign, Melania Trump denounced Biden's "socialist agenda"[69]—but what about Kamala Harris, who is usually perceived as more left than the extremely moderate Biden? Melania's husband was clear on this point: "She's a communist. She's not a socialist. She's well beyond a socialist. She wants to open up the borders to allow killers and murderers and rapists to pour into our country."[70] (Incidentally, since when are open borders a characteristic of Communism?) Biden immediately reacted: "There's not one single syllable that I've ever said that could lead you to believe

69 Michael Rubinkam, "Melania Trump Slams Biden, Dems in First Solo Campaign Stop," AP, October 27, 2020, https://apnews.com/article/melania-trump-slams-joe -biden-democrats-abea5fb241eaa7c320da7f7e22bf6342.

70 Katherine Fung, "Donald Trump Says Kamala Harris Is a 'Communist' and a 'Monster' Who Wants to Open Up Borders," Newsweek, October 8, 2020, https:// www.newsweek.com/donald-trump-says-kamala-harris-communist-monster-who -wants-open-borders-1537492.

that I was a socialist or a communist."[71] Factually true, but this rebuttal misses the point. The dismissal of Biden and Harris as socialist/communist is not simply a rhetorical exaggeration—Trump is not just saying something he knows not to be true. Rather, Trump's "exaggerations" provide an exemplary case of what one should call the *realism of notions*—the idea that notions are not just names, they structure political space and as such have actual effects. Trump's "cognitive mapping" of the political space is an almost symmetrical reversal of the Stalinist map in which everybody who opposes the Party is considered as part of a Fascist plot. In a similar way, from Trump's standpoint, the liberal center is disappearing—or, as his friend Viktor Orbán put it, liberals are just communists with a diploma[72]—which means there are only two true poles, populist nationalists and communists.

There is a wonderful expression in Serb: Ne bije al' ubija u pojam (It doesn't beat it but it kills it in the concept-notion). It refers to somebody who, instead of destroying you with direct violence, bombards you with acts that undermine your self-respect so that you end up humiliated, deprived of the very core ("notion") of your being. To "kill in a notion" describes the opposite of actual destruction (of your empirical reality) in which your "notion" survives in an elevated way (for instance, killing an enemy in such a way that they survive in the minds of thousands as a hero). This is how we should proceed with Nazism: we should not just destroy Hitler (to get rid of his "excesses" and save the sane core of his project) but kill him in his notion. And it's the same with Trump and his legacy. The true task is not just to defeat him (opening up the possibility that he will return in 2024), but to "kill him in his notion"—to make him visible in all his worthless

71 Fung, "Donald Trump Says Kamala Harris Is a 'Communist.'"

72 Kovács Zoltán, "Orbán: 'There Are No Liberals, Only Communists With University Degrees'," Index, February 17, 2020, https://index.hu/english/2020/02/17/hungary_viktor_orban_state_of_the_nation_2020/.

vanity and inconsistency, but also (and this is the crucial part) to ask how such a worthless person could have become the president of the United States. As Hegel would have put it, to kill Trump in his notion means to *bring him to his notion*, i.e., to allow him to destroy himself simply by way of making him appear as what he is.

21.

DEMOCRACY REBORN?
NOT WITH JOE BIDEN!

"Democracy reborn" (the title of a book from 2007 by the historian Garrett Epps) is used in US historiography to designate the time after the Civil War when all progressives joined forces to add Amendment XIV to the Constitution. This amendment provided African Americans with full citizenship and prohibited any state from denying any citizen equal protection under the law. It changed almost every detail of US public life, which is why scholars even call it the "Second Constitution." It was not a reconciliation between the winning North and the defeated South but a new unity imposed by the winner, a big step toward universal emancipation. Did something similar not happen in Chile with the victory of APRUEBO in the October 2020 referendum? The process of changing the constitution, which was approved by a large majority, does not aim only at getting rid of the Pinochet legacy and returning to the pre-Pinochet "democratic" era; it wants to inaugurate a more radical change, a new stage in emancipation. Here also, "democracy reborn" is not a return to some old idealized state but a radical break with the entire past.

In the Trump era, the United States was in a de facto state of ideologico-political civil war between the populist new Right and the liberal-democratic center, with even occasional threats of physical violence. Now that Trump's authoritarian populism has been defeated, is there a chance for a new "democracy reborn" in the United States? Unfortunately, this slim chance was lost with the marginalization of "democratic socialists" like Bernie Sanders and AOC. Only the alliance of Left liberals with democratic socialists could have pushed the process of democratic emancipation a step further.

With the Senate remaining in the hands of the Republicans and the Supreme Court with a conservative majority, Biden as the new president will be very restricted and will not be able to impose any serious change. Beyond this, however, the deeper problem is that Biden himself is a "moderate" agent of the economic and political establishment who is horrified of being accused of having socialist tendencies. Alexandria Ocasio-Cortez was thus fully justified when, in a post-election interview, she broke the truce and criticized the Democratic Party for incompetence, warning that if the Biden administration did not put progressives in top positions, the party would lose big in the 2022 midterm elections.[73]

The United States is now almost symmetrically divided, and Biden's words of unity and reconciliation sound vacuous. As Robert Reich put it: "How can Biden heal America when Trump doesn't want it healed?"[74] And this division is here to stay: "Trump was no accident. And the America that made him is still with us."[75] It is thus quite possible that, in the same way that the post-Civil War "rebirth of

73 Tom McCarthy, "Alexandria Ocasio-Cortez Ends Truce By Warning 'Incompetent' Democratic Party," the *Guardian*, November 8, 2020, https://www.theguardian.com/us-news/2020/nov/08/alexandria-ocasio-cortez-ends-truce-by-warning-incompetent-democratic-party.

74 Robert Reich, "How Can Biden Heal America When Trump Doesn't Want It Healed?" the *Guardian*, November 8, 2020, https://www.theguardian.com/commentisfree/2020/nov/08/joe-biden-donald-trump-election-healing-robert-reich.

75 Michael Goldfarb, "Trump Was No Accident. And the America That Made Him Is Still With Us," the *Guardian*, November 8, 2020, https://www.theguardian.com/commentisfree/2020/nov/08/trump-was-no-accident-the-america-that-made-him-is-still-with-us.

democracy" ended up in a compromise between the Republicans and anti-Black Southern Democrats, something similar will happen after a couple years of Biden rule.

But the election outcome is not just a stalemate. There is a clear winner: big capital and "deep state" apparatuses, from Google and Microsoft to the FBI and National Security Agency. From their standpoint, a weak Biden presidency with the Senate in Republican hands is the best possible outcome. Without Trump's eccentricities, international trade and political cooperation will get back to pre-Trump normality, while the Senate and Supreme Court will block any radical measures. The paradox is thus that, in the United States, the victory of the "progressive" side was at the same time its loss, a political stalemate that may even give Trump a chance to return to power in 2024.

This is why, precisely at the moment of Trump's defeat, we should ask how it was that he managed to seduce half of the American people. One reason is undoubtedly the feature that he shares with Bernie Sanders. Sanders's supporters are fiercely loyal to him—as they say, once you go Bernie you never go back. There is no mystic affection here, just a recognition by some people that Bernie really addresses them and their troubles, that he really understands them—in clear contrast to most of other Democratic candidates. It's not a matter of the realism or feasibility of Sanders's program, it is that he touches a raw nerve of his partisans. Can a voter worried about what will happen if (or, rather, when) someone in their family gets really sick seriously claim that Bloomberg or Biden really understands them?

And Trump is here superficially similar to Sanders. Although his solidarity with ordinary people is mostly limited to obscene vulgarities, he also addresses their everyday worries and fears in simple terms, giving the impression that he really cares for them and respects their dignity. One has to admit that, even in his dealing with the pandemic, Trump cunningly adopted such a "human" approach: he tried to maintain calm, telling people that the pandemic would soon be over and that they could go on with their ordinary lives . . . I've written before that Biden is Trump with a human face, more civilized and kind, but one can also say the opposite: Trump is Biden with a human face—where, of course, "humanity" is reduced to its base level of common vulgarities and insults, in the same sense that a common drunkard who babbles nonsense is more "human" that an expert talking about complex formulas.

We are now at such a low point that getting a president who will not change anything is the most we can hope for. The only group that deserves to be celebrated as heroes are those who simply ignored the violent threats of Trump's partisans and calmly went on with their job of counting votes—such praise is usually reserved for "rogue states" where a peaceful transfer of power is a cause for celebration.

The only small hope is that an unintended result of the Trump era may survive: the partial withdrawal of the United States from world politics. The United States will have to accept that it is just another state in a new multi-centric world. This is the only way for all of us to avoid the humiliating situation of fearfully following the counting of votes in the United States, as if the fate of the entire world depends on a few thousand American ignoramuses.

22.

THE STATE OF THINGS: THE CHOICE

What is our situation now with regard to the pandemic, as I write these lines at the end of November 2020, in the middle of what is called in European media "the second wave"? We should never forget that the distinction between the first and the second wave is centered on Europe. In Latin America there was a different rhythm, the peak was reached in between the two European waves, and now, as Europe suffers the second wave, the situation in Latin America is marginally better. We should also bear in mind the obvious differences in how the pandemic affects different classes (the poor are much more affected), races (in the United States, Blacks and Latinos suffer much more), sexes (women are infected more frequently and more severely than men), and how it takes different rhythms in different continents (Africa in general is less affected) and states (in Europe, France and Spain are now recovering while Germany suffers more, in clear contrast to the situation two months ago). And, especially, we should always bear in mind countries where the situation is so bad (because of war, poverty and hunger, local violence, etc.) that the pandemic is considered one of the minor evils. Just think of Yemen, on which the *Guardian* reports: "In a country stalked by disease, Covid barely registers. War, hunger and devastating aid cuts have made the plight of Yemenis almost unbearable."[76] Similarly, when the short war erupted between Azerbaijan and Armenia, officials on both sides claimed that this justified deprioritizing the struggle against the pandemic. In spite of these complications, we can nonetheless generalize some features with regard to which the contrast of the second wave and the peak of the first wave is clear:

- Some hopes are dashed now. Herd immunity doesn't work. Deaths are now at a record level in Europe. The hope no longer holds that although the virus is increasingly spreading, we have a milder variation.

- We are dealing with many unknowns, especially about how the virus is spreading. In some countries this impenetrability gave birth to a desperate search for guilty parties (gatherings in private homes or work places, secret raves, etc.). The often-heard phrase that we have to "learn to live with the virus" expresses a sense of capitulation to the virus.

- Vaccines bring hope, but we should not expect that they will magically solve all our troubles and restore the old normality, even disregarding the prospect of other epidemics and ecological catastrophes. And the distribution of vaccines will be our biggest ethical test: Will the principle of universal distribution survive, or will it be diluted through opportunist compromises?

- The model that many countries follow, that of a compromise between keeping the economy alive and fighting the pandemic, allowing it to resurge again and again (in Europe, Austria and Switzerland now want to re-open ski resorts, etc.), more and

76 Bethan McKernan, "Yemen: In a Country Stalked by Disease, Covid Barely Registers," the *Guardian*, November 27, 2020, https://www.theguardian.com/global -development/2020/nov/27/yemen-disease-covid-war.

more demonstrates its limits. The only thing that really appears to work are strict lockdowns—the latest example being the state of Victoria in Australia, which in August 2020 had 700 new cases per day, but has now "gone 30 days with no new cases of the virus, an enviable record as the U.S. and many European countries grapple with surging infections or renewed lockdowns."[77]

• With regard to mental health, we can now, in retrospect, say that most people's behavior at the peak of the first wave was a largely healthy and normal reaction to a threat. People were focused on how to avoid infection, and it was as if most of them simply didn't have time for mental health problems. Although there is much talk today about these problems, the predominant way people now relate to the pandemic is characterized by a strange mix of disparate elements. In spite of the rising number of infections, in most countries the pandemic is not quite taken seriously and there is an attitude of "life goes on," wherein it might seem that we've somehow learned to live with the virus, reflected in claims that people have "Covid fatigue." In western Europe many people are now worried about whether they will be able to celebrate Christmas and do the shopping, or take their usual winter holidays.

However, this "life goes on" stance signals quite the opposite of a moment of relaxation wherein the worst is over. It is inextricably mixed with despair, violations of state regulations, and protests against them. Since there is no clear perspective offered by the authorities or mainstream media, there is something deeper than fear at work: we've passed from fear to depression. We feel fear when there is a clear threat, and we feel frustration when obstacles emerge again and again

77 Edward Johnson, "Australia's Longest Lockdown Pays off with No Cases for 28 Days," MSN, November 27, 2020, https://www.msn.com/en-xl/news/world/australia-s-longest-lockdown-pays-off-with-no-cases-for-28-days/ar-BB1bouzN.

to prevent us from reaching what we strive for, but depression signals that our desire itself is vanishing.

What causes such a sense of disorientation is that the clear order of causality appears to us as perturbed. In Europe, for instance, for reasons that remain unclear, the numbers of infections are now falling in France and rising in Germany. Without anyone knowing exactly why, countries that were a couple of months ago held as models of how to deal with the pandemic are now its worst victims. Scientists play with different hypotheses, and this very disunity strengthens a sense of confusion and contributes to mental health crises.

What further strengthens this sense of disorientation are the many different levels on which the pandemic operates. Christian Drosten, the leading German virologist, pointed out that the pandemic is not just a scientific or health phenomenon but a natural catastrophe,[78] and one should add to this that it is also a social, economic, and ideological phenomenon—its actual effect clearly combines all of these levels. For example, CNN reports that "in Japan, more people died from suicide in November than from Covid in all of 2020. And women have been impacted most."[79] But given that the majority of these individuals committed suicide because of the predicament they were placed in by the pandemic, their deaths can be considered its collateral damage. The links between the pandemic and the economy are evident in the Western Balkans, where hospitals are being pushed over the edge. As a doctor from Bosnia said: "We can do the work of three (people), but

---

78 See Christian Drosten, "Die Pandemie Wird Jetzt Erst Richtig Losgehen. Auch Bei Uns," *Der Spiegel*, September 23, 2020, https://www.spiegel.de/wissenschaft/ medizin/christian-drosten-zu-corona-die-pandemie-wird-jetzt-erst-richtig-losgehen -auch-bei-uns-a-1b2833f0-4673-4726-a352-71ddb8bfc666.

79 Selina Wang, Rebecca Wright, and Yoko Wakatsuki, "In Japan, More People Died from Suicide Last Month Than from Covid in All of 2020," CNN, November 30, 2020, https://edition.cnn.com/2020/11/28/asia/japan-suicide-women-covid-dst -intl-hnk/index.html.

not of five."[80] One cannot understand this crisis without the "brain drain crisis, with an exodus of promising young doctors and nurses leaving to seek better wages and training abroad." The catastrophic impact of the pandemic is here clearly compounded by the emigration of the work force.

We can therefore quite safely conclude that if the Covid-19 pandemic is really to proceed in three waves, the general character of each wave will be different. In the first wave, our attention was understandably focused on our physical health, on how to prevent the virus from spreading out of control, which is why most countries accepted lockdowns and social distancing measures. Although the numbers of infected are much higher in the second wave, the fear of long-term economic consequences is nonetheless a predominant focus. And if the rollout of vaccines does not prevent a third wave, one can be sure that its focus will be on mental health, on the devastating psychic consequences of the disappearance of what we perceived as normal social life.

The ultimate alternative we are facing is: should we strive for a return to our (old) normality or should we accept that the pandemic is one of the signs that we are entering a new "post-human" era ("post-human" with regard to our predominant sense of what being human means)? This is clearly not just a choice that concerns our psychic life, but one that is in some sense "ontological," concerning our entire relation to (what we experience as) reality.

The conflicts between different ways of dealing with the pandemic are not conflicts between different medical opinions; they are serious existential ones. Here is how Brenden Dilley, a Texas chat-show host, explained why he was not wearing a mask: "Better to be dead than a

---

80 See "'Catastrophic': Balkan Health care Overwhelmed by Virus Surge," MSN, November 29, 2020, https://www.msn.com/en-xl/europe/top-stories/catastrophic -balkan-healthcare-overwhelmed-by-virus-surge/ar-BB1bsfUl.

dork. Yes, I mean that literally. I'd rather die than look like an idiot right now." Dilley refuses to wear a mask since, for him, walking around with a mask is incompatible with human dignity at its most basic level. What is at stake is thus our basic stance toward human life. Are we, like Dilley, libertarians who reject anything that encroaches upon our individual freedoms? Are we utilitarians ready to sacrifice thousands of lives for the economic well-being of the majority? Are we authoritarians who believe that only tight state control and regulation can save us? Are we New Age spiritualists who think the pandemic is a warning from Nature, a punishment for our exploitation of natural resources? Do we trust that God is just testing us and will ultimately help us to find a way out? Each of these stances relies on a specific vision of what humans are, revealing the extent to which we are all, in some sense, philosophers.

According to Giorgio Agamben, if we accept government measures implemented to fight the pandemic, we thereby abandon open social space as the core of our being-human and turn into isolated survival-machines controlled by science and technology which serve the state administration. So, even when our house is on fire, we should gather the courage to go on with life as normal and eventually die with dignity:

> Nothing I'm doing makes any sense if the house is on fire. Yet even when the house is on fire it is necessary to continue as before, to do everything with care and precision, perhaps even more so than before—even if no one notices. Perhaps life itself will disappear from the face of the earth, perhaps no memory whatsoever will remain of what has been done, for better or for worse. But you continue as before, it is too late to change, there is no time anymore.[81]

---

81 Giorgio Agamben, "When the House Is On Fire," *Ill Will*, October 27, 2020, https://illwilleditions.com/when-the-house-is-on-fire.

One should note an ambiguity in Agamben's line of argumentation: is "the house on fire" due to the pandemic (and/or the climate crisis), or is it on fire because of the way we (over)reacted to the reality of pandemic? He writes: "Today the flame has changed its form and nature, it has become digital, invisible and cold—but precisely for this very reason it is even closer still and surrounds us at every moment." These lines sound clearly Heideggerian in their location of the basic danger in the way the pandemic strengthened the ability of medical science and digital control to regulate our reaction to the pandemic.

In the very last paragraph of his text, Agamben leaves open the possibility that a new form of post-human spirituality will emerge:

> "Man disappears today, like a face in the sand erased on the shore. But what takes its place no longer has a world, only a naked life, silent and without history, at the mercy of the calculations of power and science. But perhaps it is only starting from this destruction that something else may one day slowly or suddenly appear—not a god, of course, but not even another man—a new animal, perhaps, an otherwise living soul."

Agamben refers here to the famous lines from Foucault's *Les mots et les choses* about how the humanist figure is disappearing like a figure drawn on sand washed away by the waves. We are effectively entering what can be called a post-human era, which is brought about not just by the pandemic and other catastrophes like global warming, but also by the digitalization of our lives, inclusive of direct digital access to our psychic life, which corrodes the basic coordinates of our being-human. So how can (post-)humanity be reinvented? Just one hint. In his opposition to wearing protective masks, Agamben implicitly refers to Levinas, in particular to his claim that "the face speaks to me and thereby invites me to a relation incommensurate with a power exercised," the face being the part of another's body through which the abyss of the Other's imponderable Otherness transpires.[82] Agamben's obvious conclusion is that, by way of rendering the face invisible, the protective mask renders invisible the invisible abyss itself which is echoed by a human face . . . really? There is a clear Freudian answer to this claim. Freud knew well why, in an analytic session (when it gets serious, i.e., after the so-called preliminary encounters), the patient and the analyst are not confronting each other face to face: the face is at its most basic a lie, the ultimate mask, and the analyst only accedes to the abyss of the Other by not seeing its face.

Accepting the challenge of post-humanity is our only hope. As Nicol A. Barria-Asenjo puts it in the title of her forthcoming book, instead of dreaming about a "return to (old) normality," we should engage in the difficult and painful process of constructing a new normality. This construction is not a medical or economic problem, it is a profoundly *political* one: we are compelled to invent anew our entire social life.

---

82 See Krishnan Unni P, "The Mask Is the Cultural Icon of the Pandemic," the *Indian Express,* September 24, 2020, https://indianexpress.com/article/opinion/columns/coronavirus-india-updates-death-toll-face-masks-6436379/.

23.

THE "GREAT RESET"?
YES, PLEASE—BUT A REAL ONE!

Back in April 2020, reacting to the Covid-19 outbreak, Jürgen Habermas pointed out that "existential uncertainty is now spreading globally and simultaneously, in the minds of media-networked individuals themselves."[83] He wrote: "There never was so much knowing about our not-knowing and about the constraint to act and live in uncertainty." And he was right to claim that this not-knowing not only concerns the pandemic itself—we at least have experts there—but even more its economic, social, and psychic consequences. Note his precise formulation: it is not simply that we don't know what goes on, but that we *know* that we don't know, and this not-knowing is itself a social fact, inscribed into the ways that our institutions act. We now know that in, say, medieval times or early modernity people knew much less, but they didn't know this because they relied on some stable ideological foundation which guaranteed that our universe is a meaningful totality. The same holds for some visions of Communism, even for Fukuyama's idea of the end of history—they all assumed to

---

83 Markus Schwering, "Jürgen Habermas über Corona: 'So viel Wissen über unser Nichtwissen gab es noch nie,'" *Frankfurter Rundschau*, April 10, 2020, https://www .fr.de/kultur/gesellschaft/juergen-habermas-coronavirus-krise-covid19 -interview-13642491.html. Original text: "verbreitet sich jetzt existentielle Unsicherheit global und gleichzeitig, und zwar in den Köpfen der medial vernetzten Individuen selbst . . . So viel Wissen über unser Nichtwissen und über den Zwang, unter Unsicherheit handeln und leben zu müssen, gab es noch nie."

know where history was moving. Habermas was also right to locate the uncertainty in "the minds of media-networked individuals." Our link to the wired universe tremendously expands our knowledge, but at the same time it throws us into radical uncertainty (Have we been hacked? Who controls our access? Is what we read fake news?). The ongoing discoveries about foreign hacking of US government institutions and big companies exemplify this uncertainty: Americans are now discovering that they cannot even determine the scope and methods of the hacking taking place. For the US, the viral threat is not only a biological one but also digital.

When we try to guess what our societies will look after the pandemic is over, the trap to avoid is futurology, which by definition ignores our not-knowing. Futurology is defined as a systematic forecasting of the future which extrapolates from the present trends in society, and therein resides the problem. What futurology doesn't take into account are historical "miracles," radical breaks that can only be explained retroactively, once they happen. We should perhaps mobilize here the distinction that works in French between *futur* and *avenir*. *Futur* is whatever will come after the present while *avenir* points toward a radical change. When a president wins re-election, he is "the present and future president," but he is not the president "to come"—the president to come is a different president. So will the post-Covid universe be just another future or something new "to come"?

It depends not only on science but on our *political* decisions. The time has now come to say that we should have no illusions about the "happy" outcome of the US elections, which brought such relief among liberals all around the world. John Carpenter's *They Live* (1988), one of the neglected masterpieces of the Hollywood Left, tells the story of John Nada (Spanish for "nothing"), a homeless laborer who accidentally stumbles upon a pile of boxes full of sunglasses in an abandoned church. When he puts on a pair of these glasses while walking on a street, he notices that a colorful publicity billboard soliciting us to enjoy chocolate bars now simply displays the word "OBEY," while another billboard with a glamorous couple in a tight embrace, seen through the glasses, orders the viewer to "MARRY AND REPRODUCE." He also sees that paper money bears the words "THIS IS YOUR GOD." Additionally, he soon discovers that many people who look charming are actually monstrous aliens with metal heads . . . Circulating now on the web is an image that restages this scene from *They Live* incorporating Biden and Harris. Seen directly, the image shows the two of them smiling with the message "TIME TO HEAL," but seen through the glasses, they are two alien monsters and the message is "TIME TO HEEL" . . .

This is, of course, part of the Trump propaganda to discredit Biden and Harris as puppets of anonymous corporate machines that control our lives, but there is (more than) a grain of truth in it. Biden's victory means a future continuous with the pre-Trump "normality"—that's why there was such a sigh of relief after his victory. But this "normality" means the rule of anonymous global capital, which is the true alien in our midst. I remember from my youth the desire for "socialism with a human face" against USSR-type "bureaucratic" Socialism. Biden now promises global capitalism with a human face, while behind the face the same reality will remain. In education, this "human face" assumes the form of an obsession with "well-being," according to which students should live in bubbles that shelter them from the horrors of external reality, protected by politically correct rules. Education is no longer intended to have a sobering effect that allows us to confront social reality. And when we are told that this safety will prevent mental breakdowns, we should counter it with exactly the opposite claim: such false safety makes us vulnerable to mental crises when we have to eventually confront our social reality. What this focus on "well-being" does is merely provide a false "human face" to our reality instead of enabling us to change this reality itself. Biden is the ultimate well-being president.

So why is Biden still better than Trump? Critics point out that Biden also lies and represents big capital, only in a more polite form—but, unfortunately, this form matters. With his vulgarization of public speech, Trump was corroding the ethical substance of our lives, what Hegel called *Sitten* (as opposed to individual morality). This vulgarization is a worldwide process. To give a European example, Szilard Demeter, a ministerial commissioner and head of the Petofi Literary Museum in Budapest, wrote in an op-ed in November 2020: "Europe is George Soros' gas chamber. Poison gas flows from the capsule of a multicultural open society, which is deadly to the European way of life."[84] Demeter went on to characterize Soros as "the liberal Fuhrer," insisting that his 'liber-aryan army deifies him more than did Hitler's own." If asked, Demeter would probably dismiss these statements as rhetorical exaggeration; but this in no way dismisses their terrifying implications. The comparison between Soros and Hitler is deeply anti-Semitic: it puts Soros on a level with Hitler, claiming that the multicultural open society promoted by Soros is not only as perilous as the Holocaust and the Aryan racism that sustained it ("liber-aryan") but even worse, more perilous to the "European way of life."

So is there an alternative to this terrifying vision, other than Biden's "human face"? Greta Thunberg recently articulated three positive lessons of the pandemic: "It is possible to treat a crisis like a crisis, it is possible to put people's health above economic interests, and it is possible to listen to the science."[85] Yes, but these are possi-

---

84 "Hungarian Cultural Commissioner Lights Powder Keg of Controversy after Describing Europe as 'George Soros' Gas Chamber,'" RT World News, November 29, 2020, https://www.rt.com/news/508146-soros-hungary-nazi-hitler-comparison/.

85 Suyin Haynes, "'We Now Need to Do the Impossible.' How Greta Thunberg Is Fighting for a Greener Post-Pandemic World," *Time*, December 8, 2020, https://time.com/5918448/greta-thunberg-coronavirus-climate-change/.

bilities. It's also possible to treat a crisis in such a way that one uses it to obfuscates other crises (e.g., because of the pandemic we should forget about global warming); it's also possible to use the crisis to make the rich richer and the poor poorer (as happened in 2020 with unprecedented speed); and it's also possible to ignore or compartmentalize science (e.g., those who refuse to be vaccinated, the explosive rise of conspiracy theories, etc.). Scott Galloway gives a more or less accurate picture of things in our corona time:

> We don't like to say this out loud, but I feel as if this pandemic has largely been invented for taking the top 10% into the top 1%, and taking the rest of the 90% downward. . . . We are barreling towards a nation with three million lords being served by 350 million serfs. We've decided to protect corporations, not people. Capitalism is literally collapsing on itself unless it rebuilds that pillar of empathy . . . We've decided that capitalism means being loving and empathetic to corporations, and Darwinist and harsh towards individuals.[86]

So what is Galloway's way out, how should we prevent social collapse? His solution is to put love back into capitalism through a process of creative destruction that lets failing business fail while protecting those who lose their jobs. He explains: "We let people get fired so that Apple can emerge and put Sun Microsystems out of business, and then we take that incredible prosperity and we're more empathetic with people." The problem is, of course, who is this mysterious "we"? How, exactly, is the redistribution done? Do we just

---

86 "Capitalism 'Will Collapse on Itself' Without More Empathy and Love: Scott Galloway," Yahoo Finance, December 1, 2020, https://finance.yahoo.com/news/ capitalism-will-collapse-on-itself-without-empathy-love-scott-galloway-120642769 .html; see also Scott Galloway, *Post Corona: From Crisis to Opportunity* (New York: Portfolio, 2020).

increase taxes on the winners (Apple, in this case) while allowing them to maintain their monopolist position? Galloway's idea has a certain dialectical flair: the only way to reduce inequality and poverty is to allow market competition to do its cruel job (we let people get fired), and then . . . what? Do we expect market mechanisms themselves to create new jobs? Or the state? How are "love" and "empathy" operationalized? Or do we count on the winners' empathy and expect they will all behave like Gates and Buffett? I find this supplementation of market mechanisms by morality, love, and empathy utterly problematic. Instead of enabling us to get the best of both worlds (market egotism and moral empathy), it is much more probable that we'll get the worst of both worlds.

The human face of this "leading with transparency, authenticity, and humanity" is Gates, Bezos, Zuckerberg—the faces of authoritarian corporate capitalism who all pose as humanitarian heroes, as our new aristocracy, celebrated in our media and quoted as wise humanitarians. Gates gives billions to charities, but we should remember how he opposed Elizabeth Warren's plan for a small tax increase. He praised Piketty and once almost proclaimed himself a socialist—which, in a very specific, twisted sense, we might say is true: his wealth comes from privatizing what Marx called our "commons," our shared social space in which we move and communicate. Gates's wealth has nothing to do with the production costs of the products Microsoft sells (one can even argue that Microsoft pays its intellectual workers a relatively high salary); it is not the result of his success in producing good software for lower prices than his competitors, or in higher "exploitation" of his hired intellectual workers. Gates became one of the richest men in the world through appropriating the rent from the communication platform, used by millions, that he privatized and controls. And in the same way that Microsoft privatized the communication software used by most of us, Facebook privatized our personal contacts, and Google privatized searching for information . . . The new mega-corporations that emerge through the privatization of commons justify (to some degree, at least) the idea that we are witnessing today the rise of neo-feudalism, of feudal capitalism. And by controlling our commons, the new masters (Bill Gates, Elon Musk) act in a way analogous to feudal masters. To quote Jodi Dean:

> Unlike the capitalist whose profit rests on the surplus value generated by waged workers through the production of commodities, the lord extracts value through monopoly, coercion, and rent . . . Digital platforms are the new watermills, their billionaire owners the new lords, and their thousands of workers and billions of users the new peasants.[87]

This is how Apple, Microsoft, Facebook, and Google function. We retain the freedom of our personal choice, but the scope of this choice is determined by whichever corporation privatized the particular part of our commons: we search for whatever information we need *through Google*, we freely determine our public identities *through Facebook*, etc. These mega-corporations try to colonize our future (Gates regularly proposes schemes for organizing our future lives) and even outer space (Musk owns many satellites and plans to build settlements on Mars).

There is thus a grain of truth in the Trump "rebellion" against digital corporate powers. It is worth watching the "War Room" podcasts of Steve Bannon, the greatest ideologist of Trump's populism: one cannot but be fascinated by how many partial truths he combines into an overall lie. His claim that under Obama the gap between wealthy and poor grew immensely and big corporations grew stronger is true, but under Trump this process only continued, in addition to taxes

---

87 Jodi Dean, "Neofeudalism: The End of Capitalism?" *Los Angeles Review of Books*, May 12, 2020, https://lareviewofbooks.org/article/neofeudalism-the-end-of -capitalism/.

being lowered and money being printed to bail out corporations. We are thus facing a horrible false alternative: a big corporate reset or a nationalist populism which pretends to oppose big corporations but ultimately amounts to the same. "The great reset" is the formula of how to change some things (even many things) in order that things basically remain the same.

So is there a third way, outside the two extremes of restoring the old normality and a corporate "great reset"? Yes: a true great reset. It is no secret what needs to be done—Greta Thunberg has made it clear. First, we should finally recognize the pandemic crisis for what it is: part of a global crisis of our entire way of life, from ecology to new social tensions. Second, we should establish social control and regulation over the economy. Third, we should rely on science, but without simply accepting it as the agent of decision-making. Why not? Let's return to Habermas, with whom we began: our predicament is that we are compelled to act while knowing that we don't know the full coordinates of the situation we are in, and non-acting would itself function as an act. But is this not the basic situation of every action? Our great advantage is that we *know* how much we don't know, and this knowing about our not-knowing opens up a space of freedom. We act when we don't know the whole situation, but this is not simply our limitation. What gives us freedom is that the situation—in our social sphere, at least—is in itself open, not fully (pre)determined.

Our present situation in the pandemic is certainly open. We've learned the first lesson: "lockdown light" is not enough. They tell us "we" (our economy) cannot afford another hard lockdown—so let's change the economy. Lockdown is the most radical negative gesture *within* the existing order. The way beyond, to a new positive order, leads through politics, not science. What has to be done is changing our economic life so that it will be able to survive the lockdowns and emergencies that surely await us, in the same way that a war compels us to ignore market limitations and find a way to do what is "impossible" in a free market economy.

Back in March 2003, Donald Rumsfeld, then the US secretary of defense, engaged in a little bit of amateur philosophizing about the relationship between the known and the unknown: "There are known knowns. These are things we know that we know. There are known unknowns. That is to say, there are things that we know we don't know. But there are also unknown unknowns. There are things we don't know we don't know."[88] What he forgot to add was the crucial fourth term: the "unknown knowns," things we don't know that we know—which is precisely the Freudian unconscious, the "knowledge which doesn't know itself," as Lacan used to say. If Rumsfeld thought that the main dangers in the confrontation with Iraq were the "unknown unknowns," the threats from Saddam we were not even aware of, our reply should be that the main dangers are, on the contrary, the "unknown knowns," the disavowed beliefs and suppositions we are not even aware of adhering to ourselves. We should read Habermas's claim that we have never had so much knowledge about not-knowing through these categories: the pandemic shook what we (thought we) knew that we knew; it made us aware of what we didn't know that we didn't know; and, in the way we confronted it, we relied on what we didn't know that we know (all our presumptions and prejudices that determine our actions although we are not even aware of them). We are not dealing here with the simple passage from not-knowing to knowing but with the much more subtle passage from not-knowing to knowing what we don't know—our positive knowing remains the same in this passage, but we gain a free space for action.

It is with regard to what we don't know that we know, our presumptions and prejudices, that the approach of China (and Taiwan

88 I have used this example many times in my work, most extensively in Chapter 9 of my *Defense of Lost Causes* (London: Verso Books, 2017).

and Vietnam) to the pandemic was so much better than that of Europe and the United States. I am getting tired of the eternally repeated claim "Yes, the Chinese contained the virus, but at what price?" While only a whistleblower can tell us the whole story of what really went on there, the fact is that when the virus broke out in Wuhan, the authorities imposed lockdown and halted the majority of production across the country, clearly prioritizing human lives over the economy. This happened with some delay, true, but they took the crisis extremely seriously. Now they are reaping the rewards, including economically. And—let's be clear—this was only possible because the Communist Party is still able to control and regulate the economy: there is social control over market mechanisms, albeit a "totalitarian" control. But, again, the question is not how they did it in China but how *we* should do it. The Chinese way is not the only effective way, it is not "objectively necessary" in any measurable sense. The pandemic is not just a viral process, it is a process that takes place within certain economic, social, and ideological coordinates that are open to change.

Now, at the very end of 2020, we live in a crazy time in which the hope that vaccines will work is mixed with a growing depression, despair even, due to the growing number of infections and the almost daily discoveries of new unknowns about the virus. In principle the answer to "What is to be done?" is easy here: we have the means and resources to restructure health care and economy so that they serve the needs of the people in a time of crisis. However, to quote the last line of Brecht's "In Praise of Communism" from his play *Mother*: "Er ist das Einfache, das schwer zu machen ist." ("It is the simple thing that is so hard to do.") There are many obstacles that make it so hard to do, above all the global capitalist order and its ideological hegemony. Do we then need a new Communism? Yes, but what I am tempted to call a *moderately conservative Communism*: all the steps that are necessary, from global mobilization against viral and other threats to establishing procedures to constrain market mechanisms and socialize the economy, but done in a way that is conservative (in the sense of making an effort to *conserve* the conditions of human life, which, paradoxically, will require changing things) and moderate (in the sense of carefully taking into account the unpredictable side effects of our measures).

As Emmanuel Renault pointed out, the key Marxian category that introduces class struggle into the very heart of the critique of political economy is that of the so-called "tendential laws," the laws that describe a necessary tendency in capitalist development, like the tendency of the falling rate of profit. (As Renault noted, it was already Adorno who has insisted on these dimensions of Marx's concept of *"Tendenz"* that makes it irreducible to a simple "trend.")[89] Describing this "tendency," Marx himself uses the term *antagonism*. The falling rate of profit is a tendency that pushes capitalists to strengthen workers' exploitation, and workers to resist it, so that the outcome is not predetermined but depends on the struggle—for instance, in some welfare states, organized workers forced the capitalists to make considerable concessions. The Communism I am speaking about is exactly such a tendency. The reasons for it are obvious; we need global action to fight health and environmental threats, and the economy will have to be somehow socialized. And we should read the predominant set of reactions of global capitalism to the pandemic—the fake Great Reset, nationalist populism, solidarity reduced to empathy, etc.—precisely as *a reaction to the communist tendency*.

So how will the communist tendency prevail? A sad answer: through more repeated crises. Let's make it clear: the virus is atheist in the strongest sense of the term. Yes, we should analyze how the pandemic is socially conditioned, but it is basically a product of

---

89 See T. W. Adorno, *Philosophische Elemente einer Theorie der Gesellschaft* (Frankfurt: Suhrkamp, 2008), p. 37–40.

meaningless contingency; there is no "deeper message" in it (it cannot be, for us, God's punishment, as the plague was in medieval times). Before choosing Virgil's famous line on "*acheronta movebo*" as the motto of his *Interpretation of Dreams*, Freud considered another candidate, Satan's words from Milton's *Paradise Lost*: "What reinforcement we may gain from Hope, / If not what resolution from despair." This is how we, contemporary Satans who are destroying our earth, should react to viral and ecological threats. If we are compelled to admit that our situation is hopeless, we should gain resolution from despair. We should accept that our situation is desperate, and act resolutely upon it. To quote Greta Thunberg again: "Doing our best is no longer good enough. Now we need to do the seemingly impossible." Futurology deals with what is possible; we need to do what is (from the standpoint of the existing global order) *impossible*.

24.

CHRIST IN THE TIME OF A PANDEMIC

At Christmas we commemorate the birth of Jesus Christ. What does this unique and, as Hegel put it, even monstrous event (in a grotesque disproportionality, God himself, not his messenger or prophet, appears as an ordinary person in our ordinary reality) mean to us today when a large part of humanity is crippled by a brutal pandemic and threatened by many other dangers, from global warming to social unrest? We live in some kind of hell, caught in a permanent tension and depression, the pandemic having destroyed the daily life we were used to. And here Christ enters—but how? The standard answer is that, especially in times of trouble, we should remember there is a higher almighty power which loves us and protects us, so we should turn to Him in prayer and trust in our fate. No matter how dark things are, salvation is on the horizon. And maybe God allowed the pandemic to happen in order to send us a warning . . .

I think this entire traditional line of thought should be abandoned. We should make a harder effort to grasp the unique role of Christ, which is something that escapes not only traditional Christianity but even mysticism at its best—which means, of course, Meister Eckhart. A claim sometimes attributed to Eckhart (which is not found in his work) is that he'd rather be in hell with Jesus than in heaven without him. This claim should be read not just as a hypothesis but as a real choice we have to make: the choice between God and Christ, and it is the choice between heaven and hell. As Arthur Rimbaud wrote in his *A Season in Hell* "I believe I am in hell, therefore I am." One has to take this claim in its full Cartesian sense: only in hell can I exist as a singular unique I.

Mystics progress from the temporal order of creatures to the primordial abyss of eternity, but they avoid the key question: How do creatures arise from this primordial abyss? Not "how can we reach eternity from our temporal finite being?" but "how can eternity itself descend into temporal finite existence?" The only answer is that eternity is the ultimate prison, a suffocating closure, and it is only the fall into creaturely life which introduces Opening into human (and even divine) experience. This point was made very clearly by G. K. Chesterton, who wrote apropos of the fashionable claim about the "alleged spiritual identity of Buddhism and Christianity": "Love desires personality; therefore love desires division. It is the instinct of Christianity to be glad that God has broken the universe into little pieces . . . Christianity is a sword which separates and sets free. No other philosophy makes God actually rejoice in the separation of the universe into living souls."[90] And Chesterton is fully aware that it is not enough for God to separate man from Himself so that mankind will love Him—this separation HAS to be reflected back into God Himself, so that God is abandoned *by Himself*: "When the world shook and the sun was wiped out of heaven, it was not at the crucifixion, but at the cry from the cross: the cry which confessed that God was forsaken of God." Because of this overlapping between man's isolation from God and God's isolation *from Himself*, Christianity is, Chesterton writes:

> terribly revolutionary. That a good man may have his back
> to the wall is no more than we knew already; but that God
> could have His back to the wall is a boast for all insurgents

90 G. K. Chesterton, *Orthodoxy* (San Francisco: Ignatius Press, 1995), p. 139.

for ever. Christianity is the only religion on earth that has felt that omnipotence made God incomplete. Christianity alone has felt that God, to be wholly God, must have been a rebel as well as a king.

Chesterton is fully aware that we are thereby approaching "a matter more dark and awful than it is easy to discuss." He writes: "in that terrific tale of the Passion there is a distinct emotional suggestion that the author of all things (in some unthinkable way) went not only through agony, but through doubt." In the standard form of atheism, emancipated humans stop believing in God; in Christianity, God dies *for himself*—in his "Father, why have you abandoned me?" Christ himself commits what is, for a Christian, the ultimate sin: he wavers in his Faith.

If we take seriously this paradox, we are prohibited to take refuge in the standard transcendent figure of God as a secret Master who knows the meaning of what appears to us as meaningless catastrophe; the God who sees the entire picture, in which what we perceive as a blight contributes to global harmony. When confronted with an event like the Holocaust or the death of millions in Congo in recent years, is it not obscene to claim that these horrors have a deeper meaning in that they contribute to the harmony of the Whole? Is there a Whole which can teleologically justify and thus redeem an event like the Holocaust? Christ's death on the cross signifies that one should drop without restraint the notion of God as a transcendent caretaker who guarantees the happy outcome of our acts, the guarantee of historical teleology—Christ's death is the death of *this* God, it refuses any "deeper meaning" that obfuscates the brutal reality of historical catastrophes.

This also allows us to provide the only consistent Christian answer to the eternal critical question: was God there in Auschwitz? How could He allow such immense suffering? Why didn't He intervene and prevent it? The answer is neither that we should learn to withdraw from our terrestrial vicissitudes and identify with the blessed peace of God who dwells above our misfortunes, from where we become aware of the ultimate nullity of our human concerns (the standard pagan answer), nor that God knows what he is doing and will somehow repay us for our suffering, heal our wounds, and punish the guilty (the standard teleological answer). The answer is found, for example, in the final scene of *Shooting Dogs* (released in the US as *Beyond the Gates*), in which a group of Tutsi refugees in a Christian school know that they will be shortly slaughtered by a Hutu mob. A young British teacher at the school breaks down in despair and asks his fatherly figure, the elder priest (played by John Hurt), where Christ is now to prevent the slaughter. The priest's answer is: Christ is now present here more than ever, He is suffering here with us. When we curse our fate in despair, when we courageously accept that no higher force will help us, he is here with us.

So the true message of Christmas is not, "We are safe, somebody Up There is taking care of us, he sent us his own son as his messenger!" but, "We are alone, responsible for our fate." This lack of a transcendent support is another name of freedom—Christ gives body to the divine gift of freedom. Or, as Rammstein put it in their "Ohne Dich": "Without you I cannot live, with you I am alone"—only with Christ are we truly alone. Today, we act with Christ only if we assume our responsibility for the pandemic and other catastrophes, and act together in global solidarity, aware that no higher power guarantees the happy outcome. The Christian name for this global solidarity is Holy Spirit, the community of believers bound by love. When Christ was asked by his followers how they will know of his return after his death, he answered them: when there will be love between two of you, I will be there. Christ returns as a link of love between his followers, not as a higher power uniting them.

25.

FIRST AS FARCE, THEN AS TRAGEDY?

We all know Marx's remark that history repeats itself first as a tragedy and then as a farce—Marx had in mind the tragedy of the fall of Napoleon I and the later farce of the reign of his nephew Napoleon III. Back in the 1960s, Herbert Marcuse remarked that the lesson of Nazism seems to be the opposite one: first as a farce (throughout the 1920s, Hitler and his gang were mostly taken as a bunch of marginal political clowns), then as a tragedy (when Hitler effectively took power). The storming of the US Capitol by a pro-Trump mob in January 2021 obviously wasn't a serious coup attempt but a farce. Jake Angeli, a QAnon supporter now known to many of us as the guy who entered the Capitol wearing a horned "Viking" hat, personifies the fakeness of the entire mob of protesters. Viking warriors are associated with horned helmets in popular culture, but there is no evidence that Viking helmets really had horns; such helmets were invented by early nine-teenth-century Romantic imagination—so much for the authenticity of the protesters.

What happened at the Capitol was not a coup attempt but a carnival. As Russell Sbriglia commented on the events:

Could there possibly be a better exemplification of the logic of the "theft of enjoyment" than the mantra that Trump sup-porters were chanting while storming the Capitol: "Stop the steal!"? The hedonistic, carnivalesque nature of the storming of the Capitol to "stop the steal" wasn't merely incidental to the attempted insurrection; insofar as it was all about taking back the enjoyment (supposedly) stolen from them by the nation's others (i.e., Blacks, Mexicans, Muslims, LGBTQ+, etc.), the element of carnival was absolutely essential to it.[91]

The idea that the carnival can serve as a model for progressive protest movements—with such protests being carnivalesque not only in their form and atmosphere (theatrical performances, humorous chants), but also in their non-centralized organization—is deeply problematic. Is late-capitalist social reality itself not already carnivalesque? Was the infamous *Kristallnacht* of 1938—the half-organized, half-spontaneous outburst of violent attacks on Jewish homes, synagogues, businesses, and people—not a carnival if ever there was one? Furthermore, is "carnival" not also the name for the obscene underside of power, from gang rapes to mass lynchings? Let us not forget that Michail Bakhtin developed the notion of carnival in his book on Rabelais, written in the 1930s as a direct reply to the carnival of the Stalinist purges. Traditionally, in resisting those in power, one of the strategies of the "lower classes" has regularly been to use terrifying displays of brutality to disturb the middle-class sense of decency. But with the events at the Capitol, the carnival again lost its innocence. Will, then, the farce repeat itself as tragedy in this case also? Will it be followed by a serious violent coup d'état? There are certainly ominous signs pointing in this direction:

> A poll taken the day after the assault on the Capitol revealed
> that 45 percent of Republicans approve of the action and
> believe Trump must be imposed as president by force,
> while 43 percent oppose or least do not support the use of

---

91 Russell Sbriglia (private communication).

violence to achieve this end. The Far Right has thus created a base of about 30 million people, an increasing number of whom explicitly reject the principle of democracy and are ready to accept authoritarian rule. We are lucky that the object of their veneration is crippled by narcissism and cognitive decline. It is only a matter of time, however, before a new Trump emerges, less delusional and more competent; the pathway to the installation of an authoritarian regime against the will of the majority of the electorate is now well established.[92]

Except that Trump is not crippled by narcissism and cognitive decline—these two features are at the very roots of his success. His followers' basic stance is that of a "cognitive decline": of denying the true impact of the Covid-19 pandemic, of global warming, of racism and sexism in the United States; of believing that if there are any serious threats to the American way of life, they must be the result of a conspiracy. Out of this decline emerged a substantial radical-Right movement, whose class base is (as in Fascism) a combination of lower middle-class white workers afraid of losing their privileges and their discreet billionaire enablers.

Was the US state apparatus really disturbed by the Capitol intrusion? It may seem so: "America's most senior general Mark Milley and the entire Joint Chiefs of Staff, which is comprised of the heads of each military branch, issued a statement Tuesday [January 12] condemning the violent invasion of the US Capitol last week and reminding service members of their obligation to support and defend the Constitution

---

92 Warren Montag, interview by Juan Dal Maso, "It Is Only a Matter of Time Before a More Competent Trump Emerges," *Left Voice*, January 11, 2021, https://www .leftvoice.org/the-far-right-has-never-been-so-powerful-interview-with-warren -montag.

and reject extremism."[93] There are hidden traces of solidarity between authorities and the protesters. As many noted, just imagine how much more brutal the authorities would be if BLM protesters were to lay siege on the Capitol. The protesters were not defeated, they simply went home (as Trump advised them) and congregated in a nearby bar to celebrate their act.

According to one commentator, most of the Capitol protesters "flew from their affluent suburbs to the U.S. Capitol, ready to die for the cause of white privilege."[94] This may be true, but many of them were also part of a lower-middle class that sees its privileges threatened by the imagined coalition of big business (new digital media corporations, banks), state administration (controlling our daily lives, imposing lockdowns, masks, gun control, and other limits on our basic freedoms), natural catastrophes (pandemics, forest fires), and "others" (the poor, migrants, LGBT+) who are allegedly exhausting the state's financial resources, compelling it to raise taxes. Central here is the category of "our way of life," centering upon socializing in bars and cafeterias or at large sport events, the free movement of cars, and the right to possess guns. Everything that poses a threat to these freedoms is rejected and denounced as a plot—from state control (although this is acceptable when targeting "others") and unfair Chinese trade practices, to politically correct "terror," global warming, and pandemics . . . This "way of life" is clearly not class-neutral; it is the way of life of a section of the white middle class that perceives itself as the true embodiment of "what America is about."

93 "Military Joint Chiefs Statement Condemning 'Sedition and Insurrection' at US Capitol," CNN, January 12, 2021, https://edition.cnn.com/2021/01/12/politics/joint-chiefs-memo-capitol-insurrection/index.html.

94 Will Bunch, "An Insurrection of Upper-Middle Class White People," the *Philadelphia Inquirer*, January 12, 2021, https://www.inquirer.com/columnists/attytood/capitol-breach-trump-insurrection-impeachment-white-privilege-20210112.html.

So when we hear that the agent of this conspiracy—the "deep state" dominated by liberals—did not just steal the elections but is taking from us (gradually eroding) our way of life, we should apply another category (as does Sbriglia in the above quoted comment): that of the *theft of enjoyment*. Jacques Lacan predicted in the early 1970s that capitalist globalization would give rise to a new mode of racism focused on the figure of an Other who either threatens to snatch from us our enjoyment (the deep satisfaction provided by our immersion in our way of life), and/or itself possesses and displays an excessive enjoyment that eludes our grasp (suffice it to recall the anti-Semitic fantasies about secret Jewish rituals, the white supremacist fantasies about the superior sexual prowess of Black men, or white American perceptions of Mexicans as rapists and drug dealers . . .). Enjoyment is not to be confused here with sexual or other pleasures; it is a deeper satisfaction with our specific way of life that also involves paranoia about the Other's way of life. What disturbs us about the Other is usually embodied in the small details of daily life (the smell of their food, the noise of their music or laughter). (Incidentally, was not a similar mix of fascination and horror present in the reaction of the liberal Left to the protesters breaking into the Capitol? Was not a hint of envy discernible in all the condemnation of "ordinary" people breaking into the sacred seat of power in a carnivalesque moment that momentarily suspended our rules of public life?)

The dimensions of what the pro-Trump protesters deny is terrifying. In spite of the vaccine, the Covid-19 pandemic is still spreading, with existing inequalities worsening. As for our environment, the *Guardian* reports, "the planet is facing a 'ghastly future of mass extinction, declining health and climate-disruption upheavals' that threaten human survival because of ignorance and inaction, according to an international group of scientists, who warn people still haven't grasped the urgency of the biodiversity and climate crises."[95] But what we should focus on now are the elements of another denial in Biden's inauguration ceremony. Here is SE Cupp's comment on the inauguration:

> It was almost as if none of it really happened. Except, of course it did. The last four years have tattooed a trauma on so many Americans, and it won't fade overnight. There's healing to do, and Biden has a long journey ahead. But at least for an hour or so at the United States Capitol, there was finally a much-needed respite from the madness, the moment of demarcation that will forever be 2020.[96]

Not only did Trump happen, he emerged out of the very world celebrated in "The Hill We Climb," the poem read by the young poet laureate Amanda Gorman at Biden's inauguration. Describing herself as "a skinny Black girl descended from slaves and raised by a single mother [who] can dream of becoming president only to find herself reciting for one," she said:

> "And so we lift our gaze, not to what stands between us, but what stands before us / We close the divide because we know to put our future first, we must first put our differences aside. / . . . We lay down our arms so we can reach out our arms to one another. We seek harm to none and harmony for all. / We've seen a force that would shatter our nation, rather than share it. / Would destroy our country if it meant delaying

95 Phoebe Weston, "Top Scientists Warn of 'Ghastly Future of Mass Extinction' and Climate Disruption," the *Guardian*, January 13, 2021, https://www.theguardian.com/environment/2021/jan/13/top-scientists-warn-of-ghastly-future-of-mass-extinction-and-climate-disruption-aoe.

96 SE Cupp, "Did That Really Just Happen?" CNN, January 23, 2021, https://edition.cnn.com/2021/01/20/opinions/post-inauguration-commentary/index.html.

democracy. / And this effort very nearly succeeded, but while democracy can be periodically delayed, it can never be permanently defeated in this truth."

If the term "ideology" has any meaning, this is it: the fantasy of the establishment and progressives all joined together in a sublime moment of unity. When we are immersed in this unity, it effectively appears as if none of Trump really happened—but where did Trump and his followers come from? Does his rise not signal a deep crack in that unity? If we want to have any future, we must not put our differences aside but do precisely the opposite. We must focus on the divisions and antagonisms which traverse US society—not the "uncivil war" between the liberal establishment and Trump followers, but the actual class antagonism and all its implications (racism, sexism, and the ecological crisis).

Calls for unity and healing divisions are false. Trump as such stands for radical division, for us against them (the "enemies of the people"), and the only proper way to beat him is to demonstrate that his division is a false one, that he is really one of "them" (a creature of the establishment "swamp"), and to replace this division with a more radical and true one: the establishment in all its faces against the broad unity of all emancipatory forces.

So will the farce repeat itself as tragedy? There is no advance answer to this question—it depends on all of us, on our political mobilization (or lack of it). "Be careful what you wish for!"—this was Trump's warning to Biden when the latter threatened to remove him from office by invoking the 25th Amendment.[97] Maybe Trump himself should have been more careful in wishing for the support of Far Right protesters. But he also made a pertinent point: what Biden

---

97 "'Be Careful What You Wish For': Trump Threatens Biden Over 25th Amendment," CNN, https://edition.cnn.com/videos/politics/2021/01/12/trump -alamo-border-wall-texas-remarks-vpx.cnn.

wished for—his broad vision of a new united America—is contradictory, an impossible dream, and the sooner we awaken from this dream the better for all of us. It was easy to defeat an obvious target like Trump—the real struggle begins now.

26.

WHAT IS TRUMP'S GREATEST TREASON?

When, in January 2021, district judge Vanessa Baraitser rejected the US demand to extradite Julian Assange, many leftist and liberal critics commented on this decision in terms reminiscent of the famous lines from T. S. Eliot's *Murder in the Cathedral*: "The last temptation is the greatest *treason* / To do the *right thing* for the *wrong reason*." In the play, Becket is afraid that his "right thing" (the decision to resist the king and sacrifice himself) is grounded in a "wrong reason" (his egotist search for the glory of sainthood). Hegel's answer to this predicament would be that what matters in our acts is their public content. If I enact a heroic sacrifice, this is what counts, independently of the private motifs for doing it which may be pathological.

But the rejection of the Assange extradition bid is a different case. It was obviously the right thing to do, but what is wrong are the publicly stated reasons for doing it. Judge Baraitser fully endorsed the US authorities' assertion that Assange's activities fell outside of the realm of journalism, and justified her decision purely on mental health grounds. She said: "The overall impression is of a depressed and sometimes despairing man, who is genuinely fearful about his future."[98] She added that Assange's high level of intelligence means he would probably succeed in taking his own life. Judge Baraitser's

98 Michael Holden, "UK Judge Rejects Extraditing Assange to U.S. Over 'Suicide Risk'," Reuters, https://www.reuters.com/article/uk-wikileaks-assange -idUKKBN299007.

evoking of mental health was here an excuse to deliver justice, her implicit but clear public message being: "I know the accusation is wrong, but I am not ready to admit it, so I prefer to focus on mental health." (Plus, the court also rejected bail for Assange, forcing him to remain in the conditions of imprisonment which have brought him to suicidal despair.) Assange's life is (maybe) saved, but his Cause (the freedom of the press, the struggle for the right to render public state crimes) remains a crime. This is a nice example of what the humanitarianism of our courts really amounts to.

But all this is common knowledge. What we should do is apply Eliot's lines to two other recent political events. Is the comedy that took place in Washington in early January 2021, not the final proof—if one is needed—that Assange should not be extradited to the United States? It would be like extraditing dissidents who escaped Hong Kong back to China. The first event: when Trump put pressure on Mike Pence, his vice president, not to certify electoral votes, he asked Pence to do the right thing (yes, the US electoral system is rigged and corrupted, it is one big fake organized and controlled by the "deep state") for the wrong reason. The implications of Trump's demand are interesting. He argued that Pence, instead of simply acting in his constitutionally prescribed pro forma role, could delay or obstruct the Electoral College certification set to occur in Congress.[99] After the votes were counted, the vice president had only to declare the result whose content was determined in advance—but Trump wanted Pence to act as if he was making an actual decision. What Trump demanded was not a revolution but a desperate attempt to save his day by forcing Pence to act within the institutional order, taking the letter of the law more literally than it was meant.

99 Kevin Liptak, "Pence Faces Pressure from Trump to Thwart Electoral College Vote," CNN, January 5, 2021, https://edition.cnn.com/2021/01/05/politics/mike-pence-donald-trump-electoral-college/index.html.

The second event: when pro-Trump protesters invaded the Capitol on January 6, they also did the right thing for the wrong reason. They were right in protesting the US electoral system with its complicated mechanisms whose aim is to render impossible a direct expression of popular dissatisfaction (this was clearly stated by the Founding Fathers themselves). But their attempt was not a Fascist coup. Prior to taking power, Fascists have historically tended to make a deal with big business, but now, we have news headlines like: "Trump Should Be Removed From Office to Preserve Democracy, Business Leaders Say."[100] So did Trump incite the protesters against big business? Not really. Recall that Steve Bannon was thrown out of the White House when he not only opposed Trump's tax plan but openly advocated raising taxes for the rich to 40 percent, plus he argued that rescuing banks with public money is "socialism for the rich." Trump advocating ordinary people's interests is like when Kane from Welles's classic movie, accused by a rich banker of speaking for the poor mob, answers that, yes, his newspaper speaks for poor ordinary people in order to prevent the true danger which is that *poor ordinary people will speak for themselves.*

Like any populism, today's also distrusts political representation, pretending to speak directly for the people.[101] It complains about how its hands are tied by the "deep state" and financial establishment, so its message is: "If only we didn't have our hands tied, we would be able to do away with our enemies once and for all." However, in contrast to old authoritarian populism (like Fascism) which is ready to abolish formal-representative democracy and really take over and impose a new order, today's populism doesn't have a coherent vision

---

100 Matt Egan, "Trump Should Be Removed From Office to Preserve Democracy, Business Leaders Say," CNN, January 7, 2021, https://edition.cnn.com/2021/01/06/business/capitol-hill-violence-business-leaders/index.html.

101 The uncredited quotes that follow are from Yuval Kremnitzer, "The Emperor's New Nudity: The Media, the Masses, and the Unwritten Law" (manuscript).

of some new order. The positive content of its ideology and politics is an inconsistent *bricolage* of measures to bribe "our own" poor, to lower the taxes for the rich, to focus people's hatred on the immigrants and our own corrupted elite outsourcing jobs, and so on. That's why today's populists don't really want to get rid of the established representative democracy and fully take power—"without the 'fetters' of the liberal order to struggle against, the new right would actually have to take some real action," and this would render obvious the vacuity of their program. Today's populists can only function in the indefinite postponement of achieving their goal since they can only function as opposing the "deep state" of the liberal establishment. "The new right does not, at least not at this stage, seek to establish a supreme value—for instance, the nation, or the leader—that would fully express the will of the people and thereby allow and perhaps even require the abolition of the mechanisms of representation."

What this means is that the true victims of Trump are his ordinary supporters who take seriously his babble against liberal corporate elites and big banks. His liberal critics accuse him of only seeming to control his supporters, who are ready to violently fight for him, while really being at their side, inciting them to violence. But he is *not* really on their side. On the morning of January 6, he addressed the "Save America" rally in the Ellipse, a park near the White House, saying: "We're going to walk down to the Capitol. And we're gonna cheer on our brave senators and congressmen and women. We're probably not going to be cheering so much for some of them, because you'll never take back our country with weakness, you have to show strength and you have to be strong."[102] However, when the mob did this and

---

102 Justin Vallejo, "Trump 'Save America Rally' Speech Transcript from 6 January," the *Independent*, January 13, 2021, https://www.independent.co.uk/news/world/americas/us-election-2020/trump-speech-6-january-transcript-impeachment-b1786924.html.

approached the Capitol, Trump retreated to the White House and watched on television as the violence unfolded.

Did Trump really want to make a coup d'état? Unambiguously NO. When the mob penetrated the Capitol, he made a statement: "I know your pain, I know your hurt. We had an election that was stolen from us. It was a landslide election, and everyone knows it, especially the other side. But you have to go home now. We have to have peace. We have to have law and order."[103] Trump blamed his opponents for the violence and praised his supporters, saying, "We can't play into the hands of these people. We have to have peace. So go home. We love you; you're very special." And when the mob began to disperse, Trump posted a tweet defending the actions of his supporters who stormed and vandalized the Capitol: "These are the things and events that happen when a sacred landslide election victory is so unceremoniously & viciously stripped away."[104] He concluded his tweet with: "Remember this day forever!" Yes, we should, because it displayed the fake of US democracy as well as the fake of the populist protest against it. Just a few elections in the United States have really mattered—like the California gubernatorial election in 1934, when the Democratic candidate Upton Sinclair lost because the entire establishment organized an unheard-of campaign of lies and defamations (Hollywood announced that, if Sinclair won, it would move to Florida, etc.). Trump's failure to be reelected is the opposite of Sinclair's failure: a failure of somebody who fully deserved to fail.

103 "Trump Praises Supporters as 'Very Special' after Mob Storms the Capitol," the *Guardian*, January 6, 2021, https://www.theguardian.com/us-news/live/2021/jan/06/georgia-election-latest-news-senate-ossoff-warnock-democrats-republicans-trump-biden.

104 Erik Pedersen, "Donald Trump Tweets About 'Sacred Landslide Victory'," *Deadline*, January 6, 2021, https://deadline.com/2021/01/donald-trump-speech-capitol-protest-go-home-election-was-stolen-1234666061/.

The image that will remain of the 2020 US elections is that of a furious dissatisfied crowd attacking parliament on behalf of a popular president deprived of his power through parliamentary manipulations . . . sound familiar? Yes: this should have happened in Brazil or in Bolivia—there, a crowd of supporters would have the full right to storm parliament and re-install the president. A totally different game was going on in the United States. So let's hope that what happened on January 6 in Washington will at least stop the obscenity of the United States sending observers to elections in other countries to judge their fairness—now the US elections themselves need foreign observers. The United States is a rogue country, and not just since Trump became its president: the ongoing (almost) civil war displays a rift that was there all the time.

27.

HERE'S TO YOU, JULIAN ASSANGE!

There is an old joke, from the time of World War I, about an exchange of telegrams between the German army headquarters and the Austrian-Hungarian headquarters. From Berlin to Vienna, the message is, "The situation on our part of the front is serious, but not catastrophic," and the reply from Vienna is: "With us, the situation is catastrophic, but not serious." The reply from Vienna seems to offer a model for how we tend to react to crises today, from the Covid-19 pandemic to forest fires in the West of the United States and elsewhere: we know a catastrophe is pending, the media warns us all the time, but somehow we are not ready to take the situation quite seriously.

A similar case is found in the fate of Julian Assange. His case is a legal and moral catastrophe dragging on for years. Just think of his treatment in prison: unable to see his children and their mother, unable to communicate regularly with his lawyers, and a victim of psychological torture that threatens his very survival. They are killing him softly, as the song goes. But very few seem to take his situation seriously, with an awareness that our own fate is at stake in his case. The forces that violate his rights are the forces that prevent an effective response to global warming and the pandemic. They are the forces because of which the pandemic makes the rich even richer and hits the poor hardest. They are the forces that ruthlessly exploit the pandemic to regulate and censor our social and digital spaces—the forces that protect us, including from our own freedom. We are all too ready to protest the limitations on basic human freedoms imposed in Hong Kong by China; should we not turn the gaze back on ourselves? Today, one should remember Max Horkheimer's old saying from the late 1930s: "Those who don't want to talk critically about capitalism should also keep silent about Fascism." Our version is: those who don't want to talk about the injustice done to Assange should also keep silent about the violations of human rights in Hong Kong and Belarus.

Assange's well-planned and well-executed character assassination is one of the reasons why his defense never spurred a wider movement like Black Lives Matter or Extinction Rebellion. Now that Assange's very survival is at stake, only such a movement can (perhaps) save him. Remember the lyrics (written by Joan Baez to Ennio Morricone's music) of "Here's to You," the title song of the movie *Sacco and Vanzetti*: "Here's to you, Nicola and Bart / Rest forever here in our hearts / The last and final moment is yours / That agony is your triumph." There were mass gatherings all around the world in defense of Sacco and Vanzetti, and the same is needed now in defense of Assange, although in a different form. Assange cannot die—for even if he dies (or disappears in a US prison cell like the living dead), that agony will be his triumph, he will die in order to live on in all of us. This is the message we all must deliver to those who hold his fate in their hands: if you kill a man, you create a myth that will continue to mobilize thousands.

28.

BIDEN ON PUTIN'S (LACK OF) SOUL

I am far from having any admiration for Putin or Trump, but what Joe Biden said in a recent interview with George Stephanopoulos made me almost nostalgic for some aspects of the Trump years. When Biden was asked if he believes Putin is a killer, he replied, "I do."[105] He also confirmed reports that in 2011, while serving as US vice president, he personally told Putin that the latter did not "have a soul." "I wasn't being a wise guy, I was alone with him in his office," Biden said. (What does this mean? That Putin could have killed him?) "That's how it came about. It was when President [George W.] Bush had said I've looked in his eyes and saw his soul. "I said I looked in your eyes and I don't think you have a soul. And he looked back and said, 'We understand each other.'" (What the hell was this supposed to mean? An admission from Putin that he has no soul while Biden has one? Or that they truly despise each other?) Putin's quick reply was masterful: wishing Biden good health and inviting him to a public debate about big existential and ethical issues on Zoom.

Biden's strong words stand in sharp contrast to Trump who, in 2017, when Fox News host Bill O'Reilly called Putin a "killer," suggested that America's conduct was just as bad as that of the

105 Dan Mangan, "Biden Believes Putin Is a Killer, Vows Russian Leader 'Will Pay a Price' for Trying to Help Trump Win the Election," CNBC, March 17, 2021, https://www.cnbc.com/2021/03/17/biden-says-putin-is-a-killer-will-pay-for-trying-to-help-trump-win-election.html.

Russian president. "There are a lot of killers, we've got a lot of killers," Trump said. "You think our country's so innocent?"[106] Trump displayed a dose of honest realism here. Biden's claim about Putin having no soul, on the other hand, is simply wrong. Monstrous killers do have a "soul," a rich inner life. This is seen in the way they like to produce fantasies that somehow justify their terrible acts—behind every big political crime there is a poet or a religious myth. Concretely, there is no ethnic cleansing without poetry— why? Because we live in an era that perceives itself as post-ideological. Since great public causes no longer have the force to mobilize people for mass violence, a larger sacred Cause is needed, which makes petty individual concerns about killing seem trivial. Religion or ethnic belonging fit this role perfectly. Of course there are cases of pathological atheists who are able to commit mass murder just for pleasure, but they are rare exceptions: the majority needs to be anaesthetized against their elementary sensitivity to the other's suffering, and for this, a sacred Cause is needed. Religious ideologists usually claim that, true or not, religion makes some otherwise bad people to do some good things; today, one should rather stick to Steve Weinberg's claim that while, with or without religion, good people can do good things and bad people can do bad things, only religion can make good people do bad things.

So if I am against Putin, it is not because he has no soul but because of what is in his soul. There is a passage in his 2019 interview with the *Financial Times* which exemplifies how he really speaks from his heart. Here, he solemnly declared his zero tolerance for spies who betray their country, saying: "Treason is the gravest crime possible and

---

106 Martin Pengelly, "Donald Trump Repeats Respect for 'Killer' Putin in Fox Super Bowl Interview," the *Guardian*, February 6, 2017, https://www.theguardian.com/us-news/2017/feb/05/donald-trump-repeats-his-respect-for-killer-vladimir-putin.

traitors must be punished."[107] It is clear from this outburst that Putin has no personal sympathy for Snowden or Assange; he only helps them to annoy his enemies, and one can only imagine the fate of an eventual Russian Snowden or Assange. No wonder that, in another interview, Putin said that although Snowden is not a traitor, he cannot understand how Snowden could have done what he did to his country . . . here we get a taste of Putin's soul, and of how his mind operates.

Denying that your political enemy has a soul is nothing less than a regression to vulgarity which rhymes with other of Biden's gaffes. In support of Barack Obama in 2007, for example, he said: "I mean, you got the first mainstream African-American who is articulate and bright and clean and a nice-looking guy. I mean, that's a storybook, man."[108] What these examples indicate is that if Biden's presidency is to be better than Trump's, it will not be because of his soul. The less he relies on his soul, the better for all of us.

107 Lionel Barber, Henry Foy, and Alex Barker, "Vladimir Putin Says Liberalism Has Become Obsolete," *Financial Times*, June 28, 2019, https://www.ft.com/content/670039ec-98f3-11e9-9573-ee5cbb98ed36.

108 "A Dubious Compliment – Top 10 Joe Biden Gaffes," TIME, http://content.time.com/time/specials/packages/article/0,28804,1895156_1894977_1644536,00.html.

29.

CLASS STRUGGLE AGAINST CLASSISM

At the ceremony for Joe Biden's presidential inauguration, there was a lone figure who stole the show simply by sitting there, sticking out as a discordant element disturbing the spectacle of bipartisan unity: Bernie Sanders. As Naomi Klein put it, what mattered more than his mittens was his posture:

> the slouch, the crossed arms, the physical isolation from the crowd. The effect is not of a person left out at a party but rather of a person who has no interest in joining. At an event that was, above all, a show of cross-partisan unity, Bernie's mittens stood in for everyone who has never been included in that elite-manufactured consensus.[109]

Every philosopher knows how impressed Hegel was when he saw Napoleon riding through Jena—it was for him like seeing the world spirit (the predominant historical tendency) riding a horse . . . The fact that Bernie stole the show at Biden's inauguration, and that the image of him just sitting there instantly became an icon, indicates that the true world spirit of our time was there, in his lone figure, embodying skepticism about the fake normalization staged in the ceremony. The

---

109 Naomi Klein, "The Meaning of the Mittens: Five Possibilities," the *Intercept*, January 21, 2021, https://theintercept.com/2021/01/21/inauguration-bernie -sanders-mittens/.

celebration of his image expressed that there is still hope for our cause; people are aware that radical change is needed. The lines of separation appeared clearly drawn between the liberal establishment embodied in Biden versus the democratic socialists whose most popular representatives are Bernie Sanders and Alexandria Ocasio-Cortez.

However, something happened in recent weeks which seems to disturb this clear picture. In her interviews and other public appearances, Alexandria Ocasio-Cortez engaged herself in defending Biden against attacks from the democratic socialist Left. In her interview published on March 19 in the Democratic Socialists of America's magazine *Democratic Left*, she "combines the most lavish praise for the Democratic Party with vicious denunciations of socialism."[110] As reported by Eric London, in her interview she

> presents the Democratic Party as having been completely transformed into a working class party. She says the Biden administration and incumbent Democrats are "totally reinvent[ing] themselves in a far more progressive direction." Pressure from the left has forced "almost a radical change" among entrenched Democratic leaders. . . . The only barrier to the Democratic Party establishment achieving perfection is left-wing opposition. This politician who made a career criticizing the "Democratic establishment" and posturing as an outsider has now transformed herself into the establishment's fiercest defender and a most bitter opponent of outside critics.

110 Eric London, "Alexandria Ocasio-Cortez Denounces Socialists and Praises Biden Administration, Democratic Party," World Socialist Web Site, March 25, 2021, https://www.wsws.org/en/articles/2021/03/26/aoc-m26.html.

Along these lines, AOC consequently rejects the leftist critique of Biden as a "really privileged critique,"[111] mobilizing the old and very suspicious distinction between "good faith critique" and "bad faith critique." She argues: "Bad faith critique can destroy everything that we have built so swiftly. . . . We do not have the time or the luxury to entertain bad faith actors in our movement." (Incidentally, I remember clearly this distinction from my youth when communists in power regularly opposed "constructive" criticism to destructive anti-socialist critique.) If we do not have time to "entertain bad faith actors in our movement," is this not a (not so) subtle call to a purge? AOC goes further, accusing Biden's leftist critics of betraying their disdain for the poor and oppressed by criticizing the president.[112] She also flirts with identity politics against "class essentialism," and resuscitates the old liberal-Left trick of accusing its Left critics of serving the Right: "When you say 'nothing has changed,' you are calling the people who are now protected from deportation 'no one.' And we cannot allow for that in our movement."[113] (Perhaps it is no wonder that the conflict between AOC and the democratic socialists now even involves the police, with media reports that police officers are showing up at the houses of Twitter users who criticize AOC on social media.)[114] But AOC's strategy is double here, for at the same time she criticizes the Biden administration for not going far enough in the Green New

111 Cited in London, "Alexandria Ocasio-Cortez Denounces Socialists."

112 Ibid.

113 Ibid.

114 "Police Officers Show Up at Twitter User's Home for Criticising Congresswoman AOC on Social Media, Her Spokesperson Denies Involvement," *OpIndia*, April 9, 2021, https://www.opindia.com/2021/04/usa-police-visit-twitter-user-for-criticising-congresswoman-aoc/.

Deal,[115] for not investing enough in the renewal of infrastructure,[116] and she slams Biden's "barbaric" border conditions.[117] In this way, she follows a coherent strategy: she wants the radical Left to put their trust and faith in the Biden administration, but simultaneously to exert a "good faith critique" and push it further.

The problem I see in this reasoning attributed to AOC is its implicit premise that the radical Left goes too far in the direction of "class essentialism," thereby neglecting the anti-racist and feminist progress pursued by the Biden administration. But does the Democratic Party really defend the importance of these two struggles against the radical Left? And do not some radical feminists and BLM partisans also support the Democratic establishment?[118] A part of BLM broke from the larger movement precisely because of the latter's support for the Democratic Party, or, as they put it, "to ally with the Democratic Party is to ally against ourselves."[119] The split between the Democratic

115 Danielle Kurtzleben, "Ocasio-Cortez Sees Green New Deal Progress in Biden Plan, but 'It's Not Enough,'" NPR, April 2, 2021, https://www.npr.org/2021/04/02/983398361/green-new-deal-leaders-see-biden-climate-plans-as-a-victory-kind-of.

116 Ben Winck, "AOC Says Biden's Infrastructure Plan Is Way Too Small—She Wants a $10 Trillion Package," *Business Insider*, April 1, 2021, https://www.businessinsider.com/aoc-biden-infrastructure-spending-plan-trillions-housing-health-care-recovery-2021-4.

117 Carl Campanile, "AOC Finally Slams Biden's 'Barbaric' Border Conditions, Says Families Deserve Reparations," *New York Post*, March 31, 2021, https://nypost.com/2021/03/31/aoc-slams-barbaric-us-border-conditions-under-biden/.

118 Incidentally, one should note here that the BLM elevation of white policemen shooting Blacks as the exemplary image of state violence today is not as innocent as it may appear: the fascinating force of such images of direct violence serves to obfuscate the much more dangerous and widespread racist violence which is largely invisible and enacted daily by members of the liberal establishment themselves. (I owe this insight to Angie Sparks.)

119 "'To Ally with the Democratic Party Is to Ally against Ourselves': BLM Inland Empire Breaks with BLM Global Network," *Left Voice*, February 4, 2021, https://www.leftvoice.org/blm-inland-empire-breaks-with-black-lives-matter-global-network.

establishment and the radical Left has nothing to do with the issue of class essentialism.

The first point to be made here is that, to use the old Mao Zedong's opposition, the conflict between AOC and the Democratic Left is not a "contradiction" between the people and its enemies but a contradiction within the people itself, to be resolved by debate. This means that, in our case, no side should treat the other as an agent who is secretly working for the enemy. But let's go to the basic question: who is right in this conflict—or, at least, who is less bad? I am tempted to answer this with Stalin's old formula: they are both worse. How, exactly?

In some abstract theoretical sense, the stance of the radical Left is true: Biden is not the long-term solution, and global capitalism itself is the ultimate problem. However, this insight in no way justifies what one could call a principled opportunism—the comfortable position of criticizing every modest progressive measure as inadequate and waiting for a true movement which, of course, never comes. So AOC is right in that Biden cannot simply be dismissed as "Trump with a human face" (as I've also argued). Many of the measures enacted or proposed by his administration should be supported, including the allocation of trillions of dollars toward fighting the pandemic, economic revival, and meeting ecological commitments. Another move of the Biden administration to be taken seriously is the tax reform advocated by Treasury Secretary Janet Yellen, which follows steps proposed by Thomas Piketty, increasing the US corporate tax rate from 21 percent to 28 percent, plus putting pressure on the international community to follow suit and raise taxes to a comparable level . . . This *is* "class essentialism" (a push toward economic justice) that has to be taken seriously. I agree with Chris Cillizza that the most important words in Biden's speech to the joint session of Congress on April 28,

2021, are: "My fellow Americans . . . trickle-down economics has never worked."[120]

However, if each of the opposed stances (acceptance of the Democratic Party agenda, empty leftist radicalism) is in itself wrong, does the combination of the two—the claim that we should tactically support Biden although we know his policy will not work—not amount to cynical manipulation? According to this, we officially remain within the system but in reality pursue our own, more radical and darker aims. But the truth of such a stance is usually the opposite: we think we pursue a hidden radical aim, but in reality we fit perfectly into the system, or, to quote Duane Rousselle, "it is precisely this pragmatic attempt to remain relevant, to maintain a sphere of influence within the Democratic Party, that we should question."[121] However, I do not in fact think that the strategy of supporting some of Biden's measures involves cynical manipulation, and nor does it necessarily imply that we remain caught within the system. We can support some of his measures in a totally "sincere" way, but with the presumption that they are only the first step, which will necessarily lead to further steps. And this is the case because the existing global system *cannot endure these measures without additional, radical steps*. If, for instance, spending trillions on fighting the pandemic will result in a financial crisis, then much more radical measures of financial control will be necessary. All we have to do is insist on these measures to require their full actualization.

Why, then, are both sides in the conflict worse? The heart of the matter lies in the reproach of "class essentialism" which, I think,

120 Chris Cillizza, "The Single Most Important Sentence in Joe Biden's Big Speech," CNN, April 29, 2021, https://edition.cnn.com/2021/04/29/politics/biden-speech -congress-sotu/index.html. I cannot resist noting here that these progressive measures were proposed in reaction to Trump's politics and the pandemic—i.e., they would not have happened without these. So I was right in claiming that Trump's reign and the pandemic would open up the path to more progressive politics.

121 Douane Rousselle, personal communication.

misses its target. We should of course discard the old Marxist cliché of workers' struggle being the only "real" one, according to which all other struggles (ecological, decolonization and national liberation, feminist, anti-racist, etc.) have to wait and are expected to be more or less automatically resolved once we win the Big One. But beyond this I argue that we should fully accept "class essentialism"—on condition that we use the term "essence" in the strict Hegelian sense. Although Mao Zedong did not really understand Hegel's dialectics (see his ridiculous polemic against the negation of negation), his central contribution to Marxist philosophy—his elaborations on the notion of contradiction—is at the level of Hegel's notion of essence. The main thesis of his great text *On Contradiction*, which discerns "the principal and the non-principal contradictions in a process, and the principal and the non-principal aspects of a contradiction," deserves a close reading. Mao's reproach to the "dogmatic Marxists" is that they "do not understand that it is precisely in the particularity of contradiction that the universality of contradiction resides." He writes:

> For instance, in capitalist society the two forces in contradiction, the proletariat and the bourgeoisie, form the principal contradiction. The other contradictions, such as those between the remnant feudal class and the bourgeoisie, between the peasant petty bourgeoisie and the bourgeoisie, between the proletariat and the peasant petty bourgeoisie, between the non-monopoly capitalists and the monopoly capitalists, between bourgeois democracy and bourgeois fascism, among the capitalist countries and between imperialism and the colonies, are all determined or influenced by this principal contradiction. When imperialism launches a war of aggression against such a country, all its various classes, except for some traitors, can temporarily unite in a national

war against imperialism. At such a time, the contradiction between imperialism and the country concerned becomes the principal contradiction, while all the contradictions among the various classes within the country (including what was the principal contradiction, between the feudal system and the great masses of the people) are temporarily relegated to a secondary and subordinate position.[122]

This is Mao's key point: the principal (universal) contradiction does not overlap with the contradiction which should be treated as dominant in a particular situation; the universal dimension literally *resides* in this particular contradiction. In each concrete situation, a different "particular" contradiction is the predominant one, in the precise sense that, in order to win the fight for the resolution of the principal contradiction, one should treat a particular contradiction as the predominant one, to which all other struggles should be subordinated. In China under the Japanese occupation, the patriotic unity against the Japanese was the predominant thing if the Communists wanted to win the class struggle. *In these conditions, any direct focusing on class struggle went against class struggle itself.* Therein, perhaps, resides the main feature of "dogmatic opportunism": to insist on the centrality of the principal contradiction at a wrong moment. We can immediately see how this notion applies to today's multiplicity of struggles. Today, a true "class essentialism" means treating class struggle not as a fixed essence but as an over-determining principle that regulates the dynamic interaction of multiple struggles. Today in the United States, for instance, one cannot talk about class struggle without bringing in the oppression and exploitation of Black people; to focus on "pure" class struggle independently of race ultimately serves class oppression.

122 Mao Tse-Tung, *On Practice and Contradiction* (London: Verso Books, 2010), p. 87.

Maurizio Lazzarato recently made a case against "class essential-ism,"[123] in which he refers to the Italian feminist Carla Lonzi's motto *Let's spit on Hegel.* A seminal text of Italian feminism, Lonzi's *Sputiamo su Hegel* (1970)[124] stresses the patriarchal character of Hegel's dialectic and theory of recognition, and extends this ferocious critique of Hegel to Marxism. Alongside its focus on production, hierarchical social organization and power—its location of politics in the form of a party which represents its base—Lonzi's critique takes issue with the Marxist view of history as a dialectical progression through stages, wherein Blacks and women are "blocked" at lower "stages," and women can eventually attain the freedom of self-consciousness only if they rejoin the male productivist logic.[125] Lonzi rejects this entire vision as incompatible with an authentic revolution; "the revolutionary process is a leap, a non-dialectical rupture of the order of history that will open onto the invention and discovery of something that history did not already contain."[126]

Lazzarato's point here is not that the Marxist view should be simply rejected but that workers' struggle and feminist struggle obey different logics. According to Lazzarato's interpretation of the feminist critique of "the centralization and verticality of power relations in the 'party,'" in order to become an autonomous political subject, women have to invent a radical democracy.[127] New horizontal, non-hierarchical rela-tions can provide a basis for a collective awareness specific to women. "The concept and practice of 'representation' and delegation are

123 See Maurizio Lazzarato, *Capital Hates Everyone: Fascism Or Revolution*, trans. Robert Hurley (South Pasadena, CA: Semiotext(e), 2021).

124 Accessible at http://blogue.nt2.uqam.ca/hit/files/2012/12/Lets-Spit-on-Hegel-Carla-Lonzi.pdf.

125 Lazzarato, *Capital Hates Everyone*, p. 221.

126 Ibid., p. 222.

127 Ibid., p. 218.

absent, since the problem is not the seizure, nor the management of power."[128] Women should do away with "the promises of emancipation *through work* and through *the struggle for power*, which are considered as values of the patriarchal culture (and of the workers' movement). The feminist movement doesn't demand any participation in power, but, quite the opposite, a placing into discussion of the concept of power and seizure of power."[129]

Lazzarato is aware of the traps of feminist or anti-colonialist essentialism. In the latter case, "the enemy becomes Europe as such; capitalism disappears beneath the racial division. These ambiguities will see an unfortunate reiteration in postcolonial thought, because revolution will be completely vacated."[130] So class essentialism should not be simply replaced by feminist essentialism (wherein the oppression of women is the basic form of all oppressions) or anti-colonialist essentialism (colonial domination and exploitation as the key to all others). Rather, Lazzarato asserts the irreducible plurality of struggles for emancipation, and the resonance between them. One should quote here the anonymous authors of *The Coming Insurrection*: "Revolutionary movements do not spread by contamination but by resonance / Something that is constituted here resonates with the shock wave emitted by something constituted over there . . ."[131]

How does this resonance work between feminist struggle and workers' struggle? Is workers' struggle irreducibly caught in the centralist–productivist paradigm, or can the decentralized feminist form resonate in it? And can contemporary feminism really align with an anti-colonialist respect for premodern traditions to form a

128 Ibid., p. 218.

129 Ibid., p. 222.

130 Ibid., p. 221.

131 The Invisible Committee, *The Coming Insurrection* (South Pasadena, CA: Semiotext(e), 2009), p. 12.

united front against modern organization and production? Is it not rather the case that modern feminism not only has nothing to do with premodern paradigms but is immanently antagonistic toward them? But the basic question here is: is class antagonism really just one in a series of antagonisms?

There is a nice joke from Germany about a debate between an identitarian progressive and a Marxist. The identitarian says "gender" and the Marxist replies "class." The identitarian says "gender, race" and the Marxist replies "class, class." The identitarian says "gender, race, class" and the Marxist replies "class, class, class" . . . Although the joke is supposed to make fun of the Marxist position, the Marxist is actually right; the truth in his tautology is that class (struggle) over-determines the totality of social identities.[132] When an identitarian says "ethnic identity," a Marxist analyzes how this identity is traversed by class struggle—how it is included and excluded in the social totality, which obstacles or privileges it faces, which professions and educational opportunities are open or closed to it, etc. Similarly, a Marxist analysis of the oppression of women looks at how capitalist reproduction in a country relies on their unpaid labor, to what extent their freedom and autonomy are sustained or prevented by their positioning in social and economic reproduction, and whether parts of the feminist struggle dominated by middle-class values are really feminist.

This special role of class struggle is lost when the working-class is reduced to one among other social groups whose identity has to be protected. In Germany and some other countries, one can witness the recent emergence of a vague concept of what is called "classism," essentially a class version of the politics of identity. Workers are taught to safeguard and promote their socio-cultural practices and self-respect, asserting awareness of the crucial role they play in social reproduction.

132 I owe this joke, as well as this entire line of thought, to a conversation with Arno Frank.

The workers' movement thus becomes another element in the chain of identities, like a particular ethnicity or sexual orientation. Such a "solution" of the "workers' problem" is what characterizes Fascism and populism, which accord a respect to workers and admit that they are often exploited, as well as (often sincerely) wanting to improve their position within the coordinates of the existing system. Trump, for instance, clearly advocated for the protection of US workers from banks and unfair Chinese competition.

In the domain of cinema, the latest example of such "classism" is *Nomadland* (Chloe Zhao, 2020) which portrays the daily lives of our "nomadic proletarians," workers without a permanent home who live in trailers and wander around from one temporary job to another. They are shown as decent people, full of spontaneous goodness and solidarity with each other, inhabiting their own world of small customs and rituals, enjoying their modest happiness (even the occasional work in an Amazon packaging center goes quite well . . .). That's how our hegemonic ideology likes to see workers—no wonder the movie was the big winner of the last Oscars. Although the lives depicted are rather miserable, we are bribed into enjoying the movie with the charming details of the workers' specific way of life, the underlying message being: enjoy being a nomadic proletarian!

It is precisely the refusal to be such an element in the chain of identities which defines the authentic workers' movement. In India, I met with representatives of the lowest group of the lowest caste of the Untouchables: the dry toilet cleaners. I asked them what the basic premise of their program is, what they want, and they instantly gave me the answer: "We don't want to be ourselves, what we are." We encounter here an exemplary case of what Hegel and Marx called "oppositional determination": the universal class antagonism which traverses the entire social field encounters itself as one of its species, in the class of workers who are, to quote Jacques Rancière, a "part of no-part" of the social body, lacking a proper place in it, an antagonism embodied.

So what does class struggle mean in India in May 2021, as the number of daily new Covid-19 infections in the country hits record highs? Arundhati Roy is right to claim that in India "we are witnessing a crime against humanity."[133] But the lesson here is not a simple humanitarian one, wherein we should forget political struggles and confront with all our forces the health catastrophe. To confront the health catastrophe with full force, one has to bring in many aspects of class struggle, global and local. Only now, when it is already too late, are we hearing calls for developed countries to help India. International solidarity often works like the proverbial husband who waits for his wife to do the kitchen work and then, when he is sure that the work is mostly done, generously offers his help. India was proclaimed "pharmacy of the world" for its exporting of medicines, but now that it is in need, the developed West continues with Covid nationalism instead of a an urgent, total "communist" mobilization to contain the pandemic there. We must also recognize the obvious internal causes. India "has saved the world, entire humanity, from a major tragedy by effectively controlling coronavirus," Modi boasted in January.[134] However, his nationalist politics not only criminally ignored the warnings about the danger of a new wave of infections but went on with his anti-Muslim offensive (inclusive of large public electoral meetings), and India consequently missed a unique opportunity to mobilize Hindu–Muslim solidarity in the struggle against the pandemic.

133 Arundhati Roy, "'We Are Witnessing a Crime Against Humanity': Arundhati Roy On India's Covid Catastrophe," the *Guardian*, April 28, 2021, https://www.theguardian.com/news/2021/apr/28/crime-against-humanity-arundhati-roy-india-covid-catastrophe.

134 Julia Hollingsworth, "Prime Minister Narendra Modi Could Have Prevented India's Devastating Covid-19 Crisis, Critics Say. He Didn't," CNN, May 1, 2020, https://edition.cnn.com/2021/04/30/india/covid-second-wave-narendra-modi-intl-hnk-dst/index.html.

But does the same not hold the other way around? Is class antago-nism not also traversed by racial and sexual tensions? We should reject this solution for a precise reason: there is a formal difference between class antagonism and other antagonisms. In the case of antagonisms in relations between sexes and sexual identities, the struggle for eman-cipation does not aim at annihilating some of the identities but at creating the conditions for their non-antagonistic co-existence, and the same goes for the tensions between ethnic, cultural, or religious identities—the goal is to bring about their peaceful co-existence, their mutual respect and recognition. Class struggle does not function in this way. It aims at mutual recognition and respect of classes only in its Fascist or corporatist versions. Class struggle is a "pure" antag-onism: the goal of the oppressed and exploited is to abolish classes as such, not to enact their reconciliation.[135] This is why class struggle "resonates" in other struggles in a different way than those others resonate in it—it introduces into the others an element of irreconcil-able antagonism.

So now we see why, in the conflict between AOC and radical Democratic Socialists, both sides are wrong, although they are right against each other. What the two sides share is the danger of oppor-tunism: pragmatic opportunism on the one side (the danger of getting caught in the hegemonic space, of working as its "radical" supple-ment), and principled opportunism on the other (the danger of rejecting any engagement as a compromise and in this way criticizing reality from a safe distance). What both sides miss is the proper dialec-tical unity of theory and practice in which theory not only justifies

---

135 There are two further problems to be addressed here: sexual antagonism and power. My view is that sexual antagonism is constitutive of sexuality, i.e., that there is no way to bring out a non-antagonist sexual relationship, and that relations of power and domination precede class distinction and cannot be accounted for as an effect of economic exploitation. Both patriarchy and social domination emerged earlier, with the rise of Neolithic societies—Marx missed the importance of this rupture.

particular measures but also legitimizes us to intervene "blindly" in a non-transparent situation, making us aware that the situation may change in an unpredictable way through our intervention. As Max Horkheimer said decades ago, the motto of the true radical Left should be: "Pessimism in theory, optimism in practice."

30.

"WE HAVE TO LIVE TILL WE DIE": WHAT CAN RAMMSTEIN TELL US ABOUT LIFE IN THE PANDEMIC?

One piece of wisdom the media bombard us with is that the Covid-19 pandemic has taught us about the contingency of our lives, about our mortality and biological limitation. The message is that we should abandon our dreams about dominating nature and accept our modest place in it. Is there a more sobering lesson than the one of being humiliated and reduced to near-impotence by a virus, a primitive self-reproductive mechanism which some biologists don't even count as a form of life? No wonder that calls for a new ethic of modesty and global solidarity abound . . . But is this the true lesson of the pandemic? What if the problem with our living in the shadow of the pandemic is exactly the opposite one: not death but life, a strange life that drags on, allowing us neither to live in peace nor quickly to die?

What stance toward life should we adopt in such a predicament? Maybe Rammstein's "Dalai Lama" indicates the right answer. The song is vaguely based on Goethe's "Der Erlkönig" ("King of the Elves"), a poem which tells of a father and son riding a horse when the wind begins to hypnotize the child and eventually the child dies. The child in the song is on a flight with his father; as in the poem, the travelers are menaced by a mysterious spirit which "invites" the child to join him (though only the child can hear the spirit's invitation). However, in the poem, the alarmed father rides for help, holding the child in his arms, only to find that his son is dead; in Rammstein's song, it is the father himself who causes the child's death . . . What does all this have to do with the Dalai Lama? Not only does the song make fun of the current Dalai Lama's fear of flying, but the lyrics demonstrate a more intimate link with the core of the Buddhist teaching. The Dalai Lama's fear of flying is strangely echoed in the figure of the Lord: "Man does not belong in the air, so the Lord in heaven calls his sons on the wind" to cause a strong turbulence that will kill the child. But how? Not just by crashing the plane but by directly haunting the child's soul: "A choir drips from the clouds / Crawls into the little ear / Come here, stay here / We are good to you / We are brothers to you." The Devil's voice is not a brutal cry but a soft loving whisper.

This ambiguity is crucial: the raw external threat is redoubled by a chorus of seductive voices heard only by the child. The child fights the temptation to surrender to these voices, but the father, holding him too tightly to protect him, does not notice the child's shortness of breath and "pushes the soul out of the child." (Note the ambiguous ending of the song: the lyrics never say that the plane really fell down, just that there was a strong turbulence.) The father (who obviously stands for the Dalai Lama) wants to protect the child from the external threat of reality (turbulence), but in his very excessive protection he kills his son. There is a deeper identity here between the Dalai Lama and the "king of all winds." The obvious implication is that the Buddhist protection from pain and suffering mortifies us, excludes us from life. So, to quote a well-known ironic paraphrase of the first lines of the GDR anthem, the message of "Dalai Lama" effectively is "Einverstanden mit Ruinen / Und in Zukunft abgebrannt" ("In agreement with the ruins / and in future burned down").[136]

---

136 Roberto de la Puente, "Einverstanden mit Ruinen (Agree With Ruins)," paperblog, originally published December 11, 2012, https://de.paperblog.com/

However, "Dalai Lama" gives to this standard pessimist wisdom an additional spin—the central refrain of the song is: "Weiter, weiter ins Verderben / Wir müssen leben bis wir sterben" ("Further, further into ruin / We have to live till we die"). This is what Freud called "death-drive" at its purest, not death itself but the fact that we have to *live* till we die, this endless dragging of life, this endless compulsion to repeat. The refrain is what in France they call a *lapalissade* (an empty tautological wisdom like "a minute before he died, Monsieur la Palice was still alive"). But Rammstein turns around the obvious wisdom "no matter how long you live, at the end you will die," replacing this with "till you die, you have to live." What makes the Rammstein version not an empty tautology is the ethical dimension: before we die we are not just (obviously) alive, we *have* to live. For us humans, life is a decision, an active obligation—we can lose the will to live.

This stance of "we have to live till we die" is the proper one to adopt today as the pandemic reminds all of us of our finitude and mortality; on how our life depends on an obscure interplay of (what appear to us as) contingencies. As we experience it almost daily, the true problem is not that we may die but that life just drags on in uncertainty, causing permanent depression and a loss of the will to go on. The fascination with total catastrophe and with the end of our civilization makes us spectators who morbidly enjoy the disintegration of normality; this fascination is often fed by a false feeling of guilt (the pandemic as a punishment for our decadent way of life, etc.). Now, with the promise of the vaccine and the spread of new variants of the virus, we live in an endlessly postponed breakdown. Notice how the temporal frame of the way out is changing: in the spring, authorities most often spoke of developments in terms of two-week increments ("after two weeks, it should get better"); then, in the fall of 2020, it was two months; now, it is mostly half a year (in the summer of 2021, or

einverstanden-mit-ruinen-472883/.

maybe even later, things will start to improve); some voices are already heard postponing the end of the pandemic to 2022, even 2024 . . . Every day brings news—the vaccines are working against new variants, or maybe not; the Russian Sputnik V was not good at first, but now seems to work quite well; there are big delays in the supply of vaccines, but most of us will still be vaccinated by summer . . . these endless oscillations obviously also generate a pleasure of their own, making it easier for us to survive the misery of our lives.

As in "Dalai Lama," Covid-19 is the turbulence which shattered our daily lives. What provoked the rage of today's gods? They were offended by our biogenetic manipulations and destruction of environment. But who is the Dalai Lama in our reality? For many of those who protest against lockdown and social distancing, the Dalai Lama who pretends to protect us but in reality suffocates our social freedoms are the very protective measures implemented to battle the pandemic. Giorgio Agamben recently wrote a short poem, "Si è abolito l'amore," which makes his position on these measures clear:[137]

If love is abolished / in the name of health / then health will also be abolished.

If freedom is abolished / in the name of medicine / then medicine will also be abolished.

If God is abolished / in the name of reason / then reason will also be abolished.

If man is abolished / in the name of life / then life will also be abolished.

If truth is abolished / in the name of information / information will not be abolished.

137 Giorgio Agamben, "Si è abolito l'amore," Quodlibet, November 6, 2020, https://www.quodlibet.it/giorgio-agamben-si-bolito-l-amore.

If constitution is abolished / in the name of emergency / emergency will not be abolished.

Everything is wrong with these variations on the same wisdom. First, the last two exceptions are wrong. If truth is abolished information will also be abolished because information only functions against the background of a truth, of a horizon which determines how we understand information. And if constitution is abolished then emergency will also be abolished because emergency will no longer be that but a new normality. Second, the symmetry of the first four lines is false. Love in its radical sense *is* unhealthy, as falling in love is a traumatic cut that disturbs the balance of our daily life—so it is love itself which already abolishes health. If medicine is abolished on behalf of freedom, the only freedom that remains is the freedom to die. God and reason: what reason? There is a notion of reason which doesn't need God but is far from the common naturalist determinism—just think about quantum physics . . . And what God? Agamben wrote: "What would a God be to whom neither prayers nor sacrifices were addressed?" As Lacanians, we should turn the question around: what would a sacrifice be which is not addressed to a god? Is there a sacrifice which does not presuppose some figure of the big Other? Again, Lacan's answer is: yes, the sacrifice called "symbolic castration," a sacrifice which is itself a positive act, a gesture that opens up the space for new wealth. And, finally, man and life: does the danger today not rather lie in abolishing life on behalf of man, on behalf of a certain notion of human dignity and freedom (like the ethics of war) that can lead to total self-destruction? To put my counterargument in Agamben's format: "If medicine is abolished in the name of freedom, then freedom will also be abolished. If life is abolished in the name of man, then man will also be abolished."

Rammstein's "we have to live till we die" outlines a way out of this deadlock: to fight against the pandemic not by way of withdrawing from life but by living with utmost intensity. Is there anyone more *alive* today than the millions of health care workers who, in full awareness, risk their lives on a daily basis? Many of them have died, but *till they died they were alive*. They do not just sacrifice themselves for us. And they are even less survival machines reduced to bare life. They are those who are today most alive.

31.

A EUROPEAN MANIFESTO

Some of us still remember the famous beginning of *The Communist Manifesto*: "A spectre is haunting Europe—the spectre of Communism. All the powers of old Europe have entered into a holy alliance to exorcise this spectre: Pope and Tsar, Metternich and Guizot, French Radicals and German police-spies . . ." Could we not use the same words to characterize the status of "Europe" in today's public perception? A specter is haunting the world—the specter of Eurocentrism. All the powers of old Europe and of the new world order have entered into a holy alliance to exorcise this specter: Boris Johnson and Putin, Salvini and Orbán, pro-immigrant anti-racists and protectors of traditional European values, Latino American progressives and Arab conservatives, West Bank Zionists and "patriotic" Chinese Communists . . .

Each of the opponents of Europe has its own image of Europe in mind. Boris Johnson enforced Brexit because he sees the Brussels bureaucracy as a mega-state limiting British sovereignty and the free flow of British capital, while parts of the Labour Party supported Brexit because they see Brussels bureaucracy as an instrument of international capital limiting legislation and regulations to defend workers' rights. Latino American leftists identify Eurocentrism with white colonialism, while Putin tries to dismantle the European Union to strengthen Russia's influence even beyond the ex-Soviet countries. Radical Zionists dislike Europe for being too sympathetic to

Palestinians, while some Arabs sees the European obsession with the danger of anti-Semitism as a concession to Zionism. Salvini and Orbán see the European Union as a multicultural communion that poses a threat to authentic traditional European values, opening up the gates to immigrants from foreign cultures, while immigrants see Europe as a fortress of white racism that doesn't allow them to fully integrate into it. The list goes on and on.

These critical stances toward Europe were given a boost with the pandemic. European individualism was blamed for the high number of Covid cases in Europe and contrasted with lower rates of infection in Asian countries with their stronger sense of community. The EU was perceived as inefficient, unable to organize quick vaccination, and Europe gradually succumbed to vaccine nationalism. At the same time, Europe was accused of privileging its own people and neglecting to help the impoverished Third World countries. (Here, we should at least acknowledge that the EU's delay in vaccination was the price it paid for its principled stance regarding equal distribution of the vaccine among all its members.)

One should also bear in mind that defenders of Europe are split along similar lines. We have the "technocratic" vision of Europe as another efficient actor in global capitalism, we have the liberal vision of Europe as the pre-eminent space of human rights and freedoms, and we have the conservative vision of Europe as a union of strong national identities . . . How to orient ourselves in this mess? It is all too easy to distinguish between the different aspects of Europe, the good and the bad, adopting a stance wherein we reject the Europe which gave birth to modern colonialism, racism, and slavery, but we support the Europe of human rights and multicultural openness. Such a solution recalls an American politician from the era of prohibition who, when asked where he stands on drinking wine, replies: "If you mean by wine the drink which makes an evening with friends so wonderful,

I am all for it, but if you mean by wine the horror which induces family violence and makes people jobless and degenerate, I am totally opposed to it!" Yes, Europe is a complex notion full of inner tensions, but we have to make a clear and simple decision: can "Europe" still serve as what Jacques Lacan called a Master-Signifier, as one of the names that symbolizes what the struggle for emancipation stands for?

My thesis is that it is precisely now, when Europe is in decline and the attacks on its legacy are at their strongest, that one should decide *for* Europe. The predominant target of these attacks is not Europe's racist or conservative legacies, but the emancipatory potential that is unique to Europe: secular modernity, Enlightenment, human rights and freedoms, social solidarity and justice, feminism . . . The reason we should stick with the name "Europe" is not only because good features prevail over bad; the main reason is that the European legacy itself provides the best critical instruments with which to analyze what went wrong in Europe. Are those who oppose "Eurocentrism" aware that the very terms they use in their critique are part of European legacy?

Obviously, the most visible threat to this emancipatory potential comes from within, from the new Right populism which aims at destroying the European emancipatory legacy. The Right's Europe is a Europe of nation-states bent on preserving their particular identity. When Steve Bannon visited France a couple of years ago, he made a speech which finished with the words: "God bless America and vive la France!"[138] Vive la France, viva Italia, long live Germany . . . but not Europe. We should be attentive to how this vision of Europe implies a totally different mapping of our political space.

---

138 David Reid, "Bannon Tells French Far-Right: 'Let Them Call You Racist,'" CNBC, March 12, 2018, https://www.cnbc.com/2018/03/12/steve-bannon-tells -france-right-wing-to-embrace-racist-tag.html.

Slavoj Žižek

In his *Notes Towards the Definition of Culture*, the great conservative T. S. Eliot remarked that there are moments when the only choice is the one between sectarianism and non-belief, when the only way to keep religion alive is to perform a sectarian split from its main corpse. This is our only choice today: only by means of a "sectarian split" from the standard liberal-democratic version of the European legacy, only by cutting ourselves off from the decaying corpse of the old Europe, can we keep the European legacy alive.

To act on a global scale that is not focused on Europe—for instance in helping India and others with vaccines, mobilizing internationally against global warming, and organizing global health care—is the only way to be a true European today.

32.

WHICH GAME HAS STOPPED WORKING?

One of the few flashes of spirit in our dark time is condensed in the controversy surrounding WallStreetBets, Robinhood, and GameStop. For a couple of days in late January 2021, news about the WallStreetBets controversy overshadowed the usual Big Bad news of the Covid-19 pandemic and Trump's latest antics. The story is well known, so let's recapitulate the main points Wikipedia-style. WallStreetBets (WSB) is a subreddit where millions of participants discuss stock and option trading; it is notable for its profane nature and promotion of aggressive trading strategies. Most of the members of the subreddit are young retail traders and investors or simply young amateurs who ignore fundamental investment practices and risk management techniques, so their activity is considered gambling. Many members of the subreddit use the amateur stock- and options-trading platform Robinhood, which initially offered commission-free trades of stocks and exchange-traded funds via a mobile app, before launching additional products. WSB traders rely on the price of money (interest rates) being low. The space for WSB was obviously opened up by the unprecedented uncertainty brought upon our lives by the Covid-19 pandemic: a threat of death, chaos, and social protests, while also a lot of free time due to lockdowns and quarantines.

The best-known operation of WSB traders was their unexpected massive investment in GameStop stocks. Seeing that the company was slowly losing value, the traders responded by buying up stocks, which drove prices up and caused panic and oscillations in the market. The decision to invest in GameStop was not grounded in anything that the company was doing (for instance, developing a new lucrative product); it was made just to raise the value of its stocks temporarily and then play with the oscillations. What this means is that there is a kind of self-reflexivity that characterizes WSB—what goes on in the companies that participants choose to invest in is of secondary importance; what is primary are the effects of their own activity on the market.

Critics of WSB see in such a stance a clear sign of nihilism, of reducing stock-trading to gambling. As one of the WSB participants put it: "I went from a rational investor to some sick irrational desperate gambler." This nihilism is best exemplified by the term "yolo" (you only live once), used in the WSB community to characterize people who risk their entire portfolio on a single stock or options trade. But it's not simple nihilism that motivates the WSB participants; their nihilism signals an indifference toward the final result. As Jeremy Blackburn, an assistant professor of computer science, said: "It's not even the ends that matter. It's the means. It's the fact that you're placing this bet, that's where the value in all this is. Sure, you may get money, or you may end up broke, but you played the game, and you did it in some crazy way."[139] Is this not a kind of de-alienation, a revealing of the game for what it is (in all its excess)? In his psychoanalytic theory, Jacques Lacan distinguishes between direct pleasure (enjoying the object we want) and surplus-enjoyment. His elementary example is a child sucking the mother's breast: the child does it first to satisfy his/her hunger, but then s/he begins to enjoy the act of sucking itself, and continues to do it even when there is no hunger. It's the same

139 Jon Sarlin, "Inside the Reddit Army That's Rocking Wall Street," CNN, January 30, 2021, https://edition.cnn.com/2021/01/29/investing/wallstreetbets-reddit -culture/index.html.

with shopping (many people enjoy the activity of shopping more than what they actually buy), or sexuality generally. WSB participants bring the surplus-enjoyment of stock-exchange gambling out into the open.

How does this work in our political space? WSB is a politically ambiguous populist rebellion. When Robinhood ceded to pressures and blocked retail investors from purchasing stock, Alexandria Ocasio-Cortez opposed this move with the right reason: "This is unacceptable. We now need to know more about @RobinhoodApp's decision to block retail investors from purchasing stock while hedge funds are freely able to trade the stock as they see fit."[140] (Robinhood later restored trading.) AOC was supported by Ted Cruz from the alt-Right populist standpoint of opposing big banks and Wall Street (she was right to refuse collaboration).

One can imagine the horror WSB would've inspired on Wall Street: a massive intervention in the stock market by "amateurs" who don't follow (and even don't want to know) the rules and laws of the game, and who consequently appear from the standpoint of professional investors as "irrational" lunatics spoiling the game. The key feature of the WSB community is precisely the positive function of this not-knowing: they generate shattering effects in the reality of market exchanges by ignoring the "rational" knowledge of laws and rules of investing allegedly practiced by "professional" stock-traders.

The popular appeal of WSB means that millions of ordinary people, not just high-flying financial traders, can participate in it. A new front in America's class war opened up. As Robert Reich tweeted: "So let me get this straight: Redditors rallying GameStop is market manipulation, but hedge fund billionaires shorting a stock is just

140 Tweet by Alexandria Ocasio-Cortez, https://twitter.com/AOC/status/1354830697459032066.

an investment strategy?"[141] Who would have expected this: a class war transposed into a conflict among stock investors and dealers themselves?

So it's kill the normies again, to reference the title of Angela Nagle's book. As one report explains: "For WallStreetBets, the normie culture it stands in opposition to is one of 'safe' mainstream investing: focusing on long-term gains, maxing out your 401(k)s, buying index funds."[142] But this time, the normies should really be "killed"—why? The irony is that Wall Street, the model of corrupted speculation and inside-trading, always by definition resisting state intervention and regulation, now opposes unfair competition and calls for state regulation . . . As for the accusation from Wall Street that Robinhood is a platform for gambling, suffice it to recall that Elizabeth Warren repeatedly accused hedge funds of using the stock market "like their personal casino." In short, WSB is doing openly and legally what Wall Street does in secret and illegally.

WSB's utopia of populist capitalism—the ideal of millions of ordinary people, who are workers or students by day, in the evening playing with investments—is, of course, impossible to realize; it can only end in a self-destructive chaos. But is it not in the very nature of capitalism to be periodically in crises—the Big One of 1928, the financial meltdown of 2008 (created by "rational" hedge funds!), to mention just the two best-known cases—and to come out of them strengthened? However, in both these cases, as with the WSB crisis, it was (and is) impossible to restore balance through immanent market mechanisms—the price is too high, so a massive external (state) intervention is needed. Can the state regain control of the game, restore the

---

141 Christine Romans, "Hedge Funds Bitching about Reddit Can Cry Me a River," CNN, January 29, 2021, https://edition.cnn.com/2021/01/29/investing/populist -uprising-reddit-wall-street/index.html.

142 Sarlin.

old normality ruined by WSB? The model here is China with its tight state control over the stock exchange. However, to implement this in the West would require not only a radical change in economic policy; it could only be done through a global socio-political transformation.

The excess of WSB brought into the open the latent irrationality of the stock exchange itself—it is a moment of its truth. WSB is not a rebellion against Wall Street but something potentially much more subversive. It subverts the system by over-identifying with it or, rather, by universalizing it and thereby bringing out its latent absurdity. It resembles the approach of the outsider candidate who ran in the last Croatian presidential elections—the main point of his program was: "Corruption for everybody! I promise that not only the elite will be able to profit from corruption, you all will be able to profit from it!" When placards with this slogan appeared all around Zagreb, it was the talk of the town, and people reacted with enthusiasm although they knew it was a joke . . . Yes, the January activities of the WSB participants were nihilist, but this nihilism is immanent to the stock exchange itself; it is already at work in Wall Street. To overcome this nihilism, we will have to somehow move *out* of the stock-exchange game. The moment of socialism is lurking in the background, waiting to be seized, as cracks appear in the very center of global capitalism.

Will this happen? Almost certainly not, but what should concern us is that the WSB crisis is another unexpected threat to a system already under attack from multiple sides (the pandemic, global warming, social protests . . .), and this threat comes from the very heart of the system, not from outside. An explosive mixture is in the making, and the longer the explosion is postponed, the more devastating it could be.

33.
LIGHT AT THE END OF THE TUNNEL?

We read again and again in our media that we are at the "beginning of the end" of the pandemic. Although numbers of infections and deaths are still rising, millions are already vaccinated, so that there is now at least a proverbial light at the end of the tunnel. In spite of worries about how we will survive the next few months, there are sighs of relief. We deserve this relaxation since what has been so depressing about the pandemic is precisely that there was no clear exit in sight: the feeling of the end of the world dragging on without end. Now it looks like the nightmare will soon be over; we will try to obliterate it from our memory and return to normal life as soon as possible. Some intellectuals bent on finding a deeper meaning in every catastrophe even evoke the famous verses from Friedrich Hölderlin's hymn to Patmos, "Wo aber Gefahr ist, wächst das Rettende auch" ("But where the danger is, that which saves is also growing"), as relevant for our predicament.[143] In what precisely resides this relevance? Is it simply that science saved us by inventing vaccines in record time? Is it that the pandemic reminded us of our mortality and vulnerability—we are part of nature, not its masters—and thus cured us of our arrogance?

It would be much more appropriate to turn around Hölderlin's verses: "But where that which saves us is growing, there are also

143 "Hölderlin-Trost auch in der Coronavirus-Krise: 'Wo aber Gefahr ist, wächst das Rettende auch,'" SWR2 Kulturgespräch.

dangers." These dangers are multiple—let's begin with the warning from World Health Organization experts that "even though the coronavirus pandemic has been very severe, it is 'not necessarily the big one,' and that the world will have to learn to live with Covid-19."[144] Not only is the Covid-19 pandemic far from over (infection numbers continue to rise in waves), new pandemics are on the horizon; global warming, fires, and droughts are ruining our environment; the economic effects of the pandemic will strike later, giving a new boost to public protests; and digital control of our lives will remain while mental health problems proliferate . . . We will have to learn to live not just with Covid-19 but with this entire medley of interconnected phenomena. This is why we are now going through the most dangerous moment of the entire pandemic. To relax now would be like falling asleep behind the wheel of a fast-moving car on a winding road. We have to make lots of decisions that cannot all be grounded in science. Our present moment is the moment of radical political choices.

True, science may save us; Greta Thunberg is right that we should trust it. But in a true scientific spirit we should also admit two things noted by Jürgen Habermas: with the pandemic we haven't only learned new things, we've also come to know how many things we don't know; plus, we are forced to act in such an impenetrable situation, not knowing what the effects of our acts will be.[145] As discussed above, this not-knowing not only concerns the pandemic itself, but even more its economic, social, and psychic consequences. It is not simply that we don't know what is going on, but that we *know* that we

144 Melissa Davey, "WHO Warns Covid-19 Pandemic Is 'Not Necessarily the Big One,'" the *Guardian*, December 29, 2020, https://www.theguardian.com/world/2020/dec/29/who-warns-covid-19-pandemic-is-not-necessarily-the-big-one.

145 See Markus Schwering, "Jürgen Habermas über Corona: 'So viel Wissen über unser Nichtwissen gab es noch nie,'" *Frankfurter Rundschau*, April 10, 2020, https://www.fr.de/kultur/gesellschaft/juergen-habermas-coronavirus-krise-covid19-interview-13642491.html.

don't know, and this not-knowing is itself a social fact, inscribed into the ways our institutions act.

We should even take a step further here. Today it is not just that we know more and more what we don't know; it sometimes appears as if reality itself acts as if it forgot its own laws. We know the joke about "knowledge in the real": a stone knows the law it must obey when it is falling down, etc. But the basic lesson of quantum physics is that nature itself doesn't know all its laws, and this is why Albert Einstein reacted with such anxiety to quantum physics and its basic premise of the indeterminacy of nature. For Einstein, this simply meant that quantum physics is an incomplete theory which ignores some unknown variables. There is a supreme irony in the fact that, although both Einstein and Niels Bohr were atheists, their most famous exchange is about God: Einstein remarked "God does not play dice," and Bohr snapped back, "Stop telling God what to do." Their disagreement was not about God but about the nature of our universe: Einstein couldn't accept that nature itself is in some sense "incomplete." The pandemic seems to give right to Bohr.

This indeterminacy which reaches all the way down to subatomic levels opens up the space for our interventions, but only if we fully assume it, i.e., if we reject determinism in both of its main versions: naturalism and divine providence. A Slovene theologian who advocates keeping churches open in spite of Covid quarantine regulations answered the reproach that this would cause many lives to be lost in a straightforward way: "The mission of the church is not health but salvation."[146] In short, the death and suffering of thousands doesn't matter with regard to their salvation in eternity through God . . . This is what Mother Theresa was doing in Kolkata: her mission was to take

146 "Verniki večinsko ne podpirajo nadškofovega poziva vladi, naj odpravi prepoved izvajanja verskih obredov," *Domovina*, December 16, 2020, https://www.domovina.je/verniki-vecinsko-ne-podpirajo-nadskofovega-poziva-vladi-naj-odpravi-prepoved-izvajanja-verskih-obredov/.

care of "the hungry, the naked, the homeless, the crippled, the blind, the lepers, all those people who feel unwanted, unloved, uncared for throughout society, people that have become a burden to the society and are shunned by everyone."[147] But, as critics have demonstrated, more than their health she took care of their salvation and deathbed conversion to Catholicism.[148] So we can easily imagine what she would have been doing now, as the pandemic ravages the world: no vaccinations, not even respirators, but just offering spiritual solace in a gray environment in the last hours of our lives . . . And we can also imagine what will happen in the near future if the pandemic continues to expand (i.e., through new mutations of the virus) and renders vaccines inefficient. People will be dying on a scale even more massive than in the Spanish flu and, lacking any vision of how to contain the pandemic, our authorities will resign themselves to just providing care for the dying, inclusive of pills to enable a painless death, while the Church will offer mass conversions to diminish our depression, with the promise of salvation for the faithful.

Our ultimate choice is thus best encapsulated by the beginning of a text written by Woody Allen back in 1979: "More than any other time in history, mankind faces a crossroads. One path leads to despair and utter hopelessness. The other, to total extinction. Let us pray we have the wisdom to choose correctly."[149] The correct choice is to assume despair in recognition of the utter hopelessness of our predicament—only if we pass through this zero-point will we be able to construct a new society-to-come. The wrong choice may lead us to a

147 Mother Theresa, cited in "Missionaries of Charity," Wikipedia, https:// en.wikipedia.org/wiki/Missionaries_of_Charity.

148 See Christopher Hitchens, *The Missionary Position: Mother Theresa in Theory and Practice* (London: Verso Books, 2013).

149 Woody Allen, "My Speech To the Graduates," *The New York Times*, August 10, 1979, https://www.nytimes.com/1979/08/10/archives/my-speech-to-the-graduates. html.

new divided society with the privileged living in isolated bubbles while the majority vegetates in barbaric conditions. Today, more than ever, egalitarianism is not just a vague ideal but an urgent necessity. Vaccines for all, universal health care, and a global struggle against the climate crisis are essential. There are signs that even corporations are coming to accept this. BioNTech CEO Uğur Şahin, a Turk living in Germany who played a key role in inventing the leading vaccine, said in an interview at the end of 2020: "At the moment it doesn't look good—a hole is appearing because there's a lack of other approved vaccines and we have to fill the gap with our own vaccine."[150] It is a rare and wonderful moment in late capitalism when the CEO of a company wants his competitors to get stronger because he knows that only together can they win the struggle against a global health crisis.

So maybe the proper way to conclude is to repeat the well-known warning that is sometimes added to the idea of the light at the end of the tunnel: let's make sure that this light is not the light of another train rushing toward us.

150 "Gaps in Pfizer/BioNTech Vaccine Supply Likely," the *Guardian*, January 1, 2021, https://www.theguardian.com/world/live/2021/jan/01/coronavirus-live-news-new-covid-variant-b117-in-united-states-since-october.

34.

THREE ETHICAL STANCES

Toward the beginning of his *Encyclopaedia*, Hegel speaks about the three basic stances of thinking toward objectivity (*drei Stellungen des Gedankens zur Objektivität*). To deal with the basic ethical dilemmas today, it seems appropriate to me to describe the three basic stances taken by today's intellectuals toward the topsy-turvy mess we're in.

The first stance is that of an expert who deals with the specific task imposed on him by those in power, blissfully ignoring the wider social context of his activity. Philip K. Dick's sci-fi novel *Time Out of Joint* (published back in 1959) provides an extreme version of such a constellation. It tells the story of Ragle Gumm who (thinks he) lives in 1959 in a quiet American suburb.[151] His unusual profession consists of repeatedly winning the cash prize in a local newspaper contest called "Where Will the Little Green Man Be Next?" As the novel opens, strange things begin to happen to Gumm: a soft-drink stand disappears, replaced by a small slip of paper with the words "SOFT-DRINK STAND" printed on it in block letters, plus other anomalies which signal that Gumm lives in an artificial world. A neighborhood woman invites him to a civil defense class where he sees a model of a futuristic underground military factory, and Gumm has the unshakeable feeling he's been inside that building many times

---

151 The following resume shamelessly relies on the *Time Out of Joint* entry in Wikipedia.

before . . . Confusion gradually mounts for Gumm, and the deception surrounding him (which is maintained to protect and exploit him) begins to unravel. He learns that his idyllic town is a constructed reality designed to protect him from the frightening fact that he really lives in 1998, when the Earth is at war against lunar colonists who are fighting for a permanent lunar settlement, politically independent from Earth.

Gumm has a unique ability to predict where the colonists' nuclear strikes will be aimed. Previously, Gumm did this work for the military, but then he defected to the colonists' side and planned to secretly emigrate to the Moon. But before this could happen, he began retreating into a fantasy world based largely upon the relatively idyllic surroundings of his youth. He was no longer able to shoulder his responsibility as Earth's lone protector from lunar-launched nuclear offensives. The fake town was thereby created within Gumm's mind to accommodate and rationalize his retreat into childhood so that he could continue predicting nuclear strikes in the guise of submitting entries to a harmless newspaper contest, and without the ethical qualms involved with being on the "wrong side" of a civil war. When Gumm finally remembers his true personal history, he decides to emigrate to the Moon after all because he feels that exploration and migration should never be denied to people by any government.

Gumm's predicament echoes perfectly the role of today's scientists who work for the intelligence and military establishment. Most of them inhabit the artificial, idyllic spaces of university campuses or rich suburbia, protected from the mess of contemporary life; from their standpoint, their work appears as a playful effort to resolve mathematical riddles, while the establishment uses their work to assert social control and strengthen military force.

In the novel, Gumm succeeds in breaking out of his secluded world and acquiring a critical stance that enables him to get politically engaged. But there are critical stances and critical stances, and a "radical" critical stance (the second ethical stance I propose to consider here) contains its own traps. In their "Nunca quedas mal con nadie" ("You never make a bad impression"), the Chilean band Los Prisonieros provides the perfect image of a fake "radical" leftist. Here are some of the lyrics:

> Do you think you protest? / Do you think you're some kind of rebel? / You complain about pollution / You talk about automatization / You defend humanity / You cry because the world is so bad / You critique society / You say everything should change / On the stage, you folklorize your voice / "Down with the city and its contamination" / With your cute melodies and romantic sympathy / You never make a bad impression on anyone / You tell me you protest / But . . . ! / Your position doesn't bother anyone / Is your goal to attack something, or just win applause? / You complain about the bombs / And say they will be the end of the world / But you never give any names / You're afraid to make a bad impression / You thing you're revolutionary and controversial / But you never make a bad impression / You're a bad copy of some hippie gringo / Your position, listen, you stupid beardy / Sold itself to the applause of the cheesy conscious people / You contradict all of your famous protest / With your complicated and beautiful melodies / You pretend to fight . . . / But you're just a nice piece of shit!

Although this song evokes a figure who is part of the situation in Chile, its relevance is global. I often talk about how, in today's market, we find a whole series of products deprived of their malignant property: coffee without caffeine, cream without fat, beer without alcohol . . . And the list goes on: virtual sex as sex without sex, the art of expert administration as politics without politics, up to today's tolerant liberal multiculturalism as an experience of the Other deprived of its disturbing Otherness. Los Prisonieros add another key figure from our cultural space to this series: the *decaffeinated protester*. This is a protester who says (or sings) all the right things, but somehow deprives them of their critical edge. He is horrified by global warming, he fights sexism and racism, he demands radical social change, and everyone is invited to join in the big sentiment of global solidarity—but all of this only adds up to mean that he is not required to change his life (maybe just to give to charity here and there). He goes on with his career, he is ruthlessly competitive, but he is on the right side.

In his preface to *Animal Farm*, George Orwell wrote that if liberty means anything it is "the right to tell people what they do not want to hear." This is what the decaffeinated protester never does; he gives his audience what it *wants* to hear. And what is this? The predominant attitude among academic "radical leftists" today is still the one that, back in 1937, Orwell deployed apropos class difference, writing: "We all rail against class-distinctions, but very few people seriously want to abolish them. Here you come upon the important fact that every revolutionary opinion draws part of its strength from a secret conviction that nothing can be changed."[152] Orwell's point is that radicals invoke the need for revolutionary change as a kind of superstitious token that really works to achieve the opposite; i.e., *prevents* the change from really occurring. This is seen in today's academic leftist who criticizes capitalist cultural imperialism but is in reality horrified at the idea that his field of study might disintegrate. That's why we need bands like Los Prisonieros to confront our truth with all the ruthless brutality that is required. We should gather the courage to *give names* to the evils that beset us.

152 George Orwell, *The Road to Wigan Pier* (1937), available online at http://gutenberg.net.au/ebooks02/0200391.txt.

Let's take a recent example from another part of the world of a person who "contradicts all of their famous protest with complicated and beautiful melodies." In January 2020, Jerusalem mayor Moshe Leon invited participants of the World Holocaust Forum to a one-of-a-kind cocktail party featuring a DJ in a cave underneath the Old City.[153] Only in our topsy-turvy world where obscenities are more and more a part of our daily public life could such an event be considered an appropriate conclusion to a commemoration of the Holocaust. No wonder that only days separated this event from the unveiling of another obscenity, Trump's Middle East "peace plan": a proposal for peace between two parties of which only one was consulted while the other was ignored.

Carlo Ginzburg proposed the notion that shame for one's country, not love of it, may be the true mark of belonging to it.[154] A supreme example of such shame occurred back in 2014 when hundreds of Holocaust survivors and descendants of survivors bought an ad in the *New York Times* condemning what they referred to as "the massacre of Palestinians in Gaza and the ongoing occupation and colonization of historic Palestine."[155] The statement read: "We are alarmed by the extreme, racist dehumanization of Palestinians in Israeli society, which has reached a fever-pitch." Hopefully today, more Israelis will gather the courage to feel shame apropos the politics enacted by leaders such as Netanyahu and Trump on their behalf—not, of course, shame for

153 Nir Hasson, "Jerusalem Mayor Invites Holocaust Forum Attendees to Cocktail Party," *Haaretz*, January 20, 2020, https://www.haaretz.com/israel-news/.premium -j-lem-mayor-invites-holocaust-forum-attendees-to-cocktail-party-complete-with -dj-1.8414774.

154 See Carlo Ginzburg, "The Bond of Shame," in *New Left Review* 120 (November/ December 2019), p. 35–44.

155 Matthew Kassel, "NY Times Runs Ad From Holocaust Survivors Condemning Israel, Attacking Elie Wiesel," the *Observer*, August 25, 2014, https://observer. com/2014/08/ny-times-runs-ad-from-holocaust-survivors-condemning-israel -attacking-elie-wiesel/.

being Jewish but, on the contrary, shame for what Israel's policies in the West Bank are doing to the most precious legacy of Judaism itself. This is what Los Prisonieros are telling us with "Nunca quedas mal con nadie" and other songs: sometimes, being ashamed of your country is the only way to fully belong to it and to fight for it.

What, then, would be a third stance toward the madness of the topsy-turvy world of ours, a stance which allows us to avoid the traps of the critical stance without falling back into the assertion of reality as it is? Or, in more ethical terms, how are we to go on living after we get rid of the illusions of a critical stance? In his last book, *La catastrophe ou la vie*,[156] Jean-Pierre Dupuy, *the* theorist of catastrophes (ecological, economic, etc.), collected his reflections on the Covid-19 pandemic. At the beginning of the book, he describes the challenge that the pandemic presents to his own theory of the impact of catastrophes. In this theory, he takes as a starting point Henri Bergson who, in *The Two Sources of Morality and Religion*, describes the strange sensations he experienced on August 4, 1914, when war was declared between France and Germany. Crucial here is the modality of the break between before and after. Before its outburst, the war appeared to Bergson "*simultaneously probable and impossible*: a complex and contradictory notion which persisted to the end."[157] After its outburst, it all of a sudden become real *and* possible, and the paradox resides in this retroactive appearance of probability:

> "I never pretended that one can insert reality into the past and thus work backwards in time. However, one can without any doubt insert there the possible, or, rather, at every moment, the possible insert itself there. Insofar as inpredictable and new reality creates itself, its image reflects itself behind itself

156 Jean-Pierre Dupuy, *La catastrophe ou la vie* (Paris: Editions du Seuil, 2021).

157 Henri Bergson, *Oeuvres* (Paris: PUF, 1991), pp. 1110–1111.

in the indefinite past: this new reality finds itself all the time having been possible; but it is only at the precise moment of its actual emergence that it *begins to always have been*, and this is why I say that its possibility, which does not precede its reality, will have preceded it once this reality emerges."[158]

Before the outbreak of the war, people well knew that there was a threat of military conflict, but they didn't really believe it could happen; they considered the war impossible. In our everyday epistemology, knowledge is considered higher (stronger) than belief: you believe something that you don't fully know, and full knowledge should automatically entail belief. In Bergson's case, however, you have knowledge without belief. Once the war broke out, people's stance was quickly and automatically renormalized: the war was accepted as possible. The paradox is that actuality precedes and grounds possibility: once a thing considered impossible actually happens, it becomes possible.

With the pandemic, however, things proceeded (almost) in the opposite direction. Before the pandemic broke out, its possibility and even inevitability were widely discussed; everybody was counting on it, and one can even surmise that this knowledge did not imply a lack of belief. So while the viral catastrophe was held to be possible as long as it was only foretold, when it really hit us, we couldn't really bring ourselves to believe in it. It was not "normalized" but was (and still is by many) perceived as impossible, disavowed through a range of different modalities (outright denial, conspiracy theory, and so on). One should bear in mind here the aspect of temporality: when we talk about big catastrophes like epidemics and global warming, even in a state of panic, we as a rule locate them in a not too near future (a decade or so away), as reflected in the oft-heard claim that "if we don't act now, soon it will be too late." Or, we locate the catastrophe in a

158 Bergson, *Oeuvres*, p. 1340.

faraway region (coral reefs in the north of Australia are disappearing, glaciers are melting . . .). However, the pandemic just happened—it hit us with full power and almost brought our social life to a standstill.

So what ethical stance should we adopt in such a predicament? The main obstacle to our full ethical engagement, what prevents us from actively confronting the problem, is simply fatigue. The paradox with so-called Covid fatigue is that, although it is generally thought that the obeyance of repetitive and stable customs is responsible for making life tiresome, what we are tired of these days is precisely the absence of such stable customs. We are tired of living in a permanent state of exception, awaiting new regulations from the state that tell us how to interact, unable to relax in our daily life. Many, including Rainer Paris, have published essays deploring the pandemic's ongoing destruction of everyday life, outlining the threats it poses to the routines which hold a society together.[159] One of the best Goldwynisms was when, after being informed that critics were complaining that there were too many old clichés in his films, Sam Goldwyn wrote a memo to his scenario department saying "We need more new clichés!" And this is true more generally; our most difficult task today is to create "new clichés" for ordinary daily life.

There are, of course, great cultural differences in how the prevailing sense of fatigue operates. Byung-Chul Han is right when he points out that Covid fatigue is much greater in developed Western societies because citizens there, more than elsewhere, live under the pressure of the compulsion to achieve:

> The compulsion to achieve to which we subject ourselves . . .
> accompanies us during leisure time, torments us even in our

---

159 See Rainer Paris, "Die Zerstörung des Alltags," WELT, September 23, 2020, https://www.welt.de/kultur/plus216264982/Corona-Die-Zerstoerung-des-Alltags.html.

sleep, and often leads to sleepless nights. It is not possible to recover from the compulsion to achieve. It is this internal pressure, specifically, that makes us tired. . . . The rise of egotism, atomization, and narcissism in society is a global phenomenon. Social media turns all of us into producers, entrepreneurs whose selves are the businesses. It globalizes the ego culture that erodes community, erodes anything social. We produce ourselves and put ourselves on permanent display. This self-production, this ongoing "being-on-display" of the ego, makes us tired and depressed. . . . Fundamental tiredness is ultimately a kind of ego tiredness. The home office intensifies it by entangling us even deeper in our selves. Other people, who could distract us from our ego, are missing. . . . An absence of ritual is another reason for the tiredness induced by the home office. In the name of flexibility, we are losing the fixed temporal structures and architectures that stabilize and invigorate life.[160]

One would have thought that, if depressive tiredness is caused by the way we are constantly "self-producing" in late capitalism, then the pandemic lockdown should make things easier—since we are much more socially isolated, we should experience less pressure to perform for others. Unfortunately, the effect is almost the opposite one: our business and social contacts are to a large extent transferred onto Zoom and other social media where we engage in displaying and producing ourselves even more intensely, attentive of how we appear. Spaces for socializing in which we can relax and escape the pressure to exhibit ourselves are largely eliminated. The paradox is thus that, with the lockdown and home-working conditions of the pandemic,

160 Byung-Chul Han, "The Tiredness Virus," the *Nation*, April 12, 2021, https://www.thenation.com/article/society/pandemic-burnout-society/.

our continuous "being-on-display" is in some sense strengthened: one shines with energy on Zoom, one sits tired alone at home.

So we can clearly see how even such an elementary feeling like tiredness is ultimately ideological, a result of the game of self-display that is part of our everyday ideology. Mladen Dolar[161] designated our predicament with a term borrowed from Walter Benjamin: dialectic at a standstill. This position is also one of suspense, in which we anxiously await for things to begin to move, for the New to explode. However, the feeling of standstill, the numbness and growing unresponsiveness that lead more and more people to ignore the news and to stop even caring about the future, is very deceptive; it masks the fact that we occupy a time of unprecedented social change. Since the rise of the pandemic, the global capitalist order has changed immensely—the big break that we are anxiously awaiting is already occurring.

The usual reaction to this ongoing break, the predominant form of thinking about the pandemic, is a combination of predictable motifs: with the pandemic, not only have our social and economic tensions exploded, but we've also been reminded of how we are part of nature, not its center, and we therefore have to change our way of life by limiting our individualism, developing new forms of solidarity, and accepting our modest place among life on earth. Or, as Judith Butler put it,

> an inhabitable world for humans depends on a flourishing earth that does not have humans at its center. We oppose environmental toxins not only so that we humans can live and breathe without fear of being poisoned, but also because the water and the air must have lives that are not centered on our own. As we dismantle the rigid forms of individuality in these interconnected times, we can imagine the smaller part that

161 Personal communication.

human worlds must play on this earth whose regeneration we depend upon—and which, in turn, depends upon our smaller and more mindful role.[162]

I find at least two features problematic in this fragment. First, why target "*rigid* forms of individuality"? Is the problem today not the opposite one: the prevalence of over-flexible forms of individuality ready to accommodate to ever new situations, living under permanent pressure to "reinvent" themselves again and again, experiencing every stable form as "oppressive"? Plus is it not that the pandemic is so traumatic precisely because it deprives us of fixed and reliable daily rituals?

Second, is it not too simple to insist that "the water and the air must have lives that are not centered on our own," i.e., that we have to adopt a more modest role on the earth? Global warming and other ecological threats demand of us direct collective interventions into our environment, into the fragile balance of forms of life, which will be incredibly powerful. When we say that the rise in global average temperature has to be kept below 2 degrees Celsius, we speak (and try to act) as general managers of life on earth, not as a modest species among others. The regeneration of the earth obviously does not depend upon "our smaller and more mindful role," it depends upon our gigantic role which is the truth beneath all the talk about our finitude and mortality. What we get here is the extreme form of the gap already at work in modern science and subjectivity. Modern science and subjectivity, which aim at mastering nature, are strictly co-dependent with the vision of humanity as just another species on the earth. If we have to care also about the life of water and air, it means precisely that we are what Marx called "universal beings," as it

162 Judith Butler, "Creating an Inhabitable World For Humans Means Dismantling Rigid Forms of Individuality," *TIME*, April 21, 2021, https://time.com/5953396/judith-butler-safe-world-individuality/.

were able to step outside ourselves and perceive ourselves as a minor moment of the natural totality. In premodern times when humanity perceived itself as the crown of creation, this paradoxically implied a much more modest stance.

This is the paradox we have to sustain in these crazy times: to accept that we are one among the many species on earth, and simultaneously to think and act as universal beings. To escape into the comfortable modesty of our finitude and mortality is not an option, it is a path to catastrophe.

35.

PARIS COMMUNE AT 150

In 2021 we celebrate the 150th anniversary of the Paris Commune, which lasted exactly two months and ten days (March 18–May 28, 1871). After the infamous defeat of France in the war with Germany, with the German army at the doors of Paris, the people of Paris took over and quickly organized their own power outside the coordinates of the existing state power. After the French government forces crashed the Paris Commune (and killed many Communards in the so-called "Bloody Week"), the government organized an inquest into the causes of the uprising:

> The inquest concluded that the main cause of the insurrection was a lack of belief in God, and that this problem had to be corrected immediately. It was decided that a moral revival was needed, and a key part of this was deporting 4,500 Communards to New Caledonia. There was a two-part goal in this: the government also hoped that the Communards would civilize the native Kanak people on the island, and that being exposed to the order of nature would return the Communards to the side of "good".[163]

163 "Paris Commune," Wikipedia, https://en.wikipedia.org/wiki/Paris_Commune.

The contradiction is here easy to note: the decision implies the admission that France itself is corrupted, so to return Communards to the side of the Good, they have to be isolated among (non-Christian) savages closer to nature, whom, simultaneously, they would "civilize" . . . how? With French corruption? (Is a similar inconsistency not at work in the many people dissatisfied with our corrupted civilization who seek authenticity among the less developed, but who in reality bring poison to the latter since their own notion of authenticity is projected onto them?) One can only hope that the effect was the opposite to that intended and the exiled Communards experienced solidarity with the colonized Kanaks.

From the privileged standpoint of hindsight, it is easy to claim retroactively that the Communards made virtually every mistake possible and that they were doomed to fail. But they marked a radically new beginning. The Paris Commune was the first workers' government in history, the first time modern workers took power, and this is enough to apply to it what Hegel said on the French revolution:

> Never since the sun had stood in the firmament and the planets revolved around him had it been perceived that man's existence centres in his head, *i.e.*, in Thought, inspired by which he builds up the world of reality. Anaxagoras had been the first to say that nous governs the World; but not until now had man advanced to the recognition of the principle that Thought ought to govern spiritual reality. This was accordingly a glorious mental dawn. All thinking beings shared in the jubilation of this epoch. Emotions of a lofty character stirred men's minds at that time; a spiritual enthusiasm thrilled through the world.[164]

164 G. W. F. Hegel, *The Philosophy of History*, trans. J. Sibree (Kitchener, ON: Batoche Books, 1990), https://www.marxists.org/reference/archive/hegel/works/hi/lectures4.htm.

However, the contrast between the two events immediately strikes the eye: the French Revolution aroused sublime feelings in the public all around Europe (recall the famous description of this effect by Kant), while the Paris Commune was mostly met by horror. After the Commune was defeated, "enlightened" writers from George Sand to Gustave Flaubert visited the trials of the Communards to see the cases of degenerated humanity, Nietzsche dismissed the Commune as the last slave rebellion, etc.—the honorable exception was here the old Victor Hugo who fought for the amnesty of the imprisoned Communards. The continuity between the French Revolution and the Commune is at another level. The reception among the enlightened public of the first phase of the French Revolution was enthusiastic, and this enthusiasm turned into horror when the Jacobins took over: 1789 yes, 1793 no. At the level of political dynamic, the Commune was the reappearance of 1793—but not a precise one. Something happened with the Commune that did not happen in 1793.

Although praised by Marx as "the form at last discovered" for the overcoming of state and the emancipation of the proletariat, i.e., as the first taste of how the "dictatorship of the proletariat" will look, we should note that the Commune was a surprise for Marx himself. We tend to forget that Marxists were a minority in the Commune. With his triumphant interpretation of the Commune in *The Civil War in France*, written during and immediately after the Commune, Marx reappropriated an event in which his followers were marginalized by the anarchist, Proudhonist, and Bakuninist majority. Plus, the popular base of the Commune was not just workers but also artisans, small owners, etc. The figure whom Communards themselves perceived as their leader was Louis Auguste Blanqui, a French revolutionary socialist who was more concerned with the revolution itself than with the future society that would result from it. Contrary to Marx, Blanqui did not believe in the preponderant role of the working class, nor in popular movements; he thought that the revolution should be carried out by a small group, who would establish a temporary dictatorship by force. This period of transitional tyranny would permit the implementation of the basis of a new order, after which power would be handed to the people—in short, Blanqui was a Leninist *avant la lettre*.

On March 17, 1871, Adolphe Thiers, acting head of the French government in the confused state after the defeat in the war against Germany, aware of the threat represented by Blanqui, had him arrested. A few days later, the insurrection that established the Paris Commune broke out, and Blanqui was elected president of the insurgent commune. The Communards offered to release all of their prisoners if the Thiers government released Blanqui, but their offer was met with refusal. Marx himself, in spite of his critique of Blanqui, was convinced that Blanqui was the leader that was missed by the Commune. Blanqui was not focused on the program of a revolution; he aimed at forming an organized group that would smash the state and take power—no wonder that Lenin himself danced in the snow in a Kremlin court when Bolshevik power lasted a day longer than the Commune. But was the Bolshevik regime a true heir of the Commune? Yes, they first legitimized their reign with the slogan "All power to the soviets (local councils)!" but then they quickly disbanded them.

So why was Marx surprised by the Commune? What did he learn from it? Before the Commune, he conceived of the revolution as a set of measures executed by a central power (nationalization of banks, free universal health care and education, etc., enumerated at the end of the *Communist Manifesto*). The "surprise" of the Commune was the local self-organization of the people, its attempt at a democracy which grows from below, from local councils, with active participation of the people. (The Jacobins did not make this step which, in their case, would have meant dismantling the National Assembly—which is why they lost power by a simple vote in the assembly.)

Can the Commune still be a model for us today? When the predominant form of political representation is exhausted, can our political engagement be given new life through the direct awakening of the people? Yes, but the harsh lesson of history is that the difficult point comes afterward, when popular enthusiasm has to be transformed into an effective political organization with a precise program. Recall the "chaotic" leaderless and decentralized character of the *gilet jaunes* (yellow vests) protests in France. One can claim that this, precisely, was their strength, aiding them to expose the gap between ordinary experience and political representation. Instead of a clear agent addressing demands to the state and thereby offering itself as a partner in dialogue, we get a polymorphous popular pressure, and what puts those in power in a panic is precisely that this pressure cannot be localized in a clear opponent but remains a version of what Antonio Negri calls "multitude." If such a pressure expresses itself in concrete demands, these demands are not what the protest is really about . . . However, at some point, hysterical demands have to translate themselves into a political program (or they disappear). The protesters' demands are the expression of a deeper dissatisfaction with the very liberal-democratic capitalist order in which demands can only be met through the process of parliamentary political representation. In other words, the protests contain a deeper demand for a different logic of economico-political organization, and here a new leader is needed to operationalize this deeper demand.

The solution is not that somehow the self-organized and mobilized civil society directly takes over and replaces the state. Direct rule of the multitude is an illusion; as a rule it has to be sustained in a strong state apparatus.

In Trump's inauguration speech in 2017 he said: "Today's ceremony has very special meaning, because today we are not merely transferring power from one administration to another, or from one party

Slavoj Žižek

to another, but we are transferring power from Washington, D.C., and giving it back to you, the people."[165] Till now elites were ruling, but: "That all changes, starting right here and right now, because this moment is your moment—it belongs to you. It belongs to everyone gathered here today, and everyone watching, all across America. This is your day." We should not take these words just as a cheap demagoguery but as an indication of what is wrong in the very idea of the direct power of the people. In a Blanquist way, people did try to take power by invading the Capitol in January 2021. Of course, the "people" were in this case the white middle class whose privileges were threatened; but their actions responded to a deeper crisis of representation.

Is the solution here some kind of return to the Commune with its vision and practice of direct democracy? Should we oppose the "false" Capitol crowd and the "authentic" *gilets jaunes* crowd? Maybe what we are witnessing today, with "post-truth" politics, is the end of the entire idea of a true and authentic people's will that is usually manipulated and misrepresented but for whose adequate representation we should strive. The way to beat Trumpian populism is not to claim that it doesn't really stand for the people, and that the real people's will should be allowed to express itself outside this populism. The very fact that people's will can be "manipulated" in such a thorough way signals its fantasmatic character. In a Hegelian way, the critique of representation should thus be inverted into the critique of what representation is supposed to represent. To get this point, we should draw a parallel not between the Commune and today's situation, but between today and the French revolution of 1848. Recall Marx's deservedly famous description of the political position of peasants as a class from his writings on the 1848 revolution:

165 "2017 Donald Trump Inauguration Speech Transcript," January 20, 2017, POLITICO, https://www.politico.com/story/2017/01/full-text-donald-trump-inauguration-speech-transcript-233907.

The smallholding peasants form a vast mass, the members of which live in similar conditions but without entering into manifold relations with one another. Their mode of production isolates them from one another instead of bringing them into mutual intercourse. . . . In this way, the great mass of the French nation is formed by the simple addition of homologous magnitudes, much as potatoes in a sack form a sack of potatoes. . . . They cannot represent themselves, they must be represented. Their representative must at the same time appear as their master, as an authority over them, as an unlimited government power that protects them against the other classes and sends them rain and sunshine from above. The political influence of the smallholding peasants, therefore, finds its final expression in the executive power subordinating society to itself.[166]

And was it not the same in Egypt when the Arab Spring protests, with their demand for adequate political representation, overthrew the Mubarak regime and brought in democracy? But with democracy, those unrepresented went to vote and brought to power the Muslim Brotherhood, while the participants in the popular protests, mostly the educated middle-class youth, with their agenda of freedom, were marginalized. Today the problem of representation is exploding also in the developed Western countries. Whole strata don't represent themselves—they even actively reject being represented since they perceive as fake the very form of representation—and when they mobilize it is under the banner of a populist leader. Maybe this is one of the succinct definitions of populism: the movement of those who do not trust political representation. What Marx said for the French

166 Karl Marx, "The Eighteenth Brumaire of Louis Bonaparte," in *Marx and Engels Selected Works* (Moscow: Foreign Languages Publishing House, 1955), vol. 1.

peasant protests of 1848 fits perfectly the attack on the Capitol: "Their entry into the revolutionary movement, clumsily cunning, knavishly naïve, doltishly sublime, a calculated superstition, a pathetic burlesque, a cleverly stupid anachronism, a world-historic piece of buffoonery and an undecipherable hieroglyph for the understanding of the civilized—this symbol bore the unmistakable physiognomy of the class that represents barbarism within civilization."[167] The "revolutionary" attackers were clumsily cunning (thinking they are deceiving anyone by their rhetoric), knavishly naïve (in following Trump as the embodiment of popular freedom), and doltishly sublime (evoking the great tradition of the founding fathers betrayed by the US administration). They acted on a calculated superstition (not really believing in their conspiracy theories they relied on), displayed a pathetic burlesque (imitating revolutionary fervor), and represented a cleverly stupid anachronism (defending the old American values of freedom) . . . As such, they were truly "an undecipherable hieroglyph": an explosion of anti-Enlightenment barbarism that brought forth the hidden antagonisms of our civilization.

This anti-Enlightenment thrust that characterizes our time is often captured in the term "post-truth era." A recent incident that occurred in the US legal system brings us to the core of this weird phenomenon. In March 2021, Dominion Voting Systems filed a defamation lawsuit against the pro-Trump right-wing attorney Sidney Powell over her claims that the company, which manufactured electronic voting machines used by some districts in the 2020 election, changed votes for President Trump to votes for President-Elect Biden (in addition to her claim that this company had links with the regime of the late Hugo Chávez in Venezuela). Powell's defense against the lawsuit was

167 Karl Marx, "The Class Struggles in France, 1848 to 1850," in *Selected Works*, vol. 1 (Moscow: Progress Publishers, 1969), https://www.marxists.org/archive/marx/works/1850/class-struggles-france/ch02.htm.

uncanny—in a new court filing, she claimed that reasonable people wouldn't have believed as fact her assertions of fraud after the 2020 presidential election:

> Indeed, Plaintiffs themselves characterize the statements at issue as "wild accusations" and "outlandish claims." They are repeatedly labelled "inherently improbable" and even "impossible." Such characterizations of the allegedly defamatory statements further support Defendants' position that reasonable people would not accept such statements as fact but view them only as claims that await testing by the courts through the adversary process.[168]

The underlying logic is that statements are really defamatory (and one can be prosecuted for them) if they could be taken seriously by at least some reasonable people. So if the problematic statements are characterized as "outlandish" and "improbable," i.e., if no reasonable person can take them seriously, they are not a defamation and one cannot be prosecuted for them . . . One can imagine a defense of Hitler framed in the same terms, i.e., that his idea of a Bolshevik–Jewish plot was so outlandish and improbable that no reasonable person could take it seriously . . . The problem is that millions died because of that outlandish idea. And something similar (although not, of course, of the same weight) holds for Powell: statements such as hers mobilized millions, brought the United States closer to the brink of a civil war, and caused deaths.

The underlying question is: If, when Powell was spreading her defamations, she was aware that all reasonable people would see they

168 Katelyn Polantz, "Sidney Powell Argues in New Court Filing that No Reasonable People Would Believe Her Election Fraud Claims," CNN, March 23, 2021, https://edition.cnn.com/2021/03/22/politics/sidney-powell-dominion-lawsuit-election-fraud/index.html.

were ridiculous and false, *why was she then doing it?* To manipulate and seduce the unreasonable crowd by way of mobilizing our irrational instincts? Things are more complicated here: yes, Powell was aware that she had no rational grounds for her defamations, she was knowingly spreading non-truths, but it was as if she fell into her own trap and identified with what she knew was not true. She was not a manipulator exempting herself from her lies: *she was in exactly the same position as her "victims."*

Her defamations have the status of rumors, but they are rumors elevated into the public discourse. Powell exemplifies the new era in which rumors openly operate in public space and form a social link.[169] Her mode of fetishist disavowal is the obverse of the traditional one with regard to public dignity of a person ("I know that our leader has private sins, but I will act as if he is without them to save his dignity"): "although I don't really know if these rumors are true, I will spread them as if they are true . . .".

Decades ago, I encountered a similar logic when I was caught in a ferocious debate with an anti-Semite who defended the truth of the "Protocols of Zion" (the description of the secret Jewish plan to dominate the world fabricated around 1900 by the Russian Tsarist secret police). I pointed out how it was convincingly proven that they were fabricated (numerous factual mistakes in the text make it clear beyond doubt that they are a fake). But the anti-Semite insisted that the Protocols were authentic, and, in answer to the obvious reproach that there are mistakes in the text, argued that Jews *themselves* introduced mistakes to make it appear that the Protocols were a forgery, so that gentiles would not take them seriously, while those in the know would be able to use them as a guideline free of suspicions.

169 See "Four Reflections On Power, Appearance, And Obscenity," in Slavoj Žižek, *Pandemic! 2: Chronicles of a Time Lost* (New York, NY: OR Books, 2020).

What the crazy anti-Semite imagined, Sidney Powell is trying to sell us as a fact. She is dismissing what she herself said as outlandish and improbable, not to be taken seriously, *making sure that her words will continue to have real effects.* This is how ideology functions in our post-truth era. Today, when we are caught in the process of a gradual disintegration of the public common space, we can no longer rely on the trust in the people, on the trust that, if we only give the people the chance to break the spell of ideological manipulations, they will arrive at their substantial truth. Here we encounter the fatal limitation of the much-praised "leaderless" character of the French protests, of their chaotic self-organization: it is not enough for a leader to listen to the people and formulate their interests and wants into a program. The old Henry Ford was right to ignore what people wanted when he developed the serially produced car. As he put it succinctly, if asked what they want, the people would answer: "A better and stronger horse to pull our carriage!" And the same goes for a political leader that is needed today. The *gilets jaunes* protesters want a better (stronger and cheaper) horse—in this case, ironically, cheaper fuel for their cars. They should be given the vision of a society where the price of fuel no longer matters in the same way that after the introduction of cars the price of horse fodder no longer mattered.

But this, of course, is only one aspect of being a true leader. The other, opposite one is the ability to make tough decisions where they cannot be avoided: which group of soldiers to sacrifice on a battle-field, which patient to let die when there are not enough resources, etc. As an old doctor in the TV series *New Amsterdam* says: "Leaders make choices that keep them awake at night. If you sleep well, you are not one of them." Paradoxically, the excess that cannot be captured by mechanisms of electoral political representation can only find adequate expression in a leader or a leading body that is able to impose a long-term social and economic project and is not constrained by the narrow period between two elections . . . Does this sound like universal militarization? Yes, the forthcoming Communism will be a war Communism or there will be none.[170]

This is how we should reflect on the legacy of the Commune today: instead of getting lost in nostalgic memories, we should focus on how to imagine a popular mobilization today, in the conditions of a dispersed working class traversed by many conflicting interests. As Hegel was fully aware, a Leader (or a leading collective body) does not reflect some substantial content that pre-exists it, namely "the true will of the people." A true Leader literally *creates* the People as a united political agent out of a confused mess of inconsistent tendencies. When, in the summer of 1953, workers' protests erupted in East Berlin, Brecht wrote a short poem "The Solution":

After the uprising of the 17th of June
The Secretary of the Writers' Union
Had distributed leaflets on the Stalinallee
Stating that the people
Had forfeited the confidence of the government
And could only win it back
By increased work quotas. Would it not in that case be
simpler
for the government
To dissolve the people
And elect another?

This poem is usually read as a sarcastic denouncement of the Party's arrogance, but what if we take it as a realist description of what happens in every truly radical emancipatory process in which

170 For a more detailed argumentation, see Fredric Jameson et al., ed. Slavoj Žižek, *An American Utopia: Dual Power and the Universal Army* (London: Verso Books, 2016).

the leadership literally recreates the people, "elects" another people as a disciplined political force? We have to renounce the dream or hope that, at some point, feminism, anti-racism, LGBT+ struggles, protection of minorities, worker's struggles, freedom of expression struggles, hate-speech opponents, freedom of information efforts, etc., will join into one big Movement in which trans-feminists will march together with Muslim women, in which students who feel their intellectual freedom is constrained protest with workers whose wages don't allow them to survive. Along these lines, Alain Badiou complained that in the Occupy Wall Street protests and those in 2011 in Turkey and Egypt, protesters mostly came from the educated middle classes and didn't mobilize the silent working class. Apropos OWS and the *gilets jaunes* in France, he goes a step further and claims that the working class in the developed Western world is already part of what Lenin called the "workers aristocracy" which is prone to racism, corrupted by the ruling class, and deprived of any emancipatory potential, such that it is no longer an ally. The dream of the famous scene in 1968 when students went to a Renault factory to meet with workers there is over; we should, rather, try to establish a link between jobless precarious intellectuals, dissatisfied students, and immigrants . . . What lurks behind these efforts is a desperate search for today's incarnation of a true emancipatory agent that would replace Marx's working class. Badiou's candidate is "nomadic proletarians."

With the loss of a substantial reference to the people, one should finally abandon the myth of the Commune's innocence—as if the Communards were communists before the Fall (the "totalitarian" terror of the twentieth century), as if in the Commune the dream of direct cooperation was realized with no alienated intermediary structures, even if people were effectively eating rats . . . What if, in contrast to the obsession with how to overcome the alienation of state institutions and bring about a self-transparent society, our proper task today is almost the opposite one: to enact a "good alienation," to invent a different mode of *passivity* of the majority? The formula of the mobilization of a crowd is a political version of Freud's *Wo Es war, soll Ich werden* (where it was, shall I be): where the chaotic crowd was, the party organization should come—or, as Hegel would have put it, where the chaotic popular substance brews, the well-organized subject should impose order and direction. But today we should add another spin to this formula and move from subject back to substance—to a different substance created by the subject, to a new social order in which we can dwell with trust and pursue our lives.

36.

WHY I AM STILL A COMMUNIST

I am the first to admit that the communist dream of the twentieth century is over. And my position is as far as imaginable from the old stupid mantra that Communism was a good idea that just got corrupted by totalitarian perverts. No, there are problems already in the original vision, so one should submit to a severe reassessment of Marx himself too. Yes, communists in power did some good things. We know the litany—education, health, the fight against Fascism—but overall their only real triumph is what happened in China after 1980, arguably the greatest economic success story in human history, where hundreds of millions were raised from poverty into middle-class existence. How did China achieve it? The twentieth-century Left was defined by its opposition to two fundamental tendencies of modernity: the reign of capital with its aggressive individualism and alienating dynamics, and authoritarian-bureaucratic state power. What we get in today's China is exactly the combination of these two features in its extreme form—a strong authoritarian state, wild capitalist dynamics—and this is the most efficient form of socialism today . . . But is this what I want?

China today is becoming the model of what Henry Farrell called "networked authoritarianism." The idea is that

> if a state spies on people enough and allows machine-learning systems to incorporate their behavior and respond to it, it is possible to create "a more efficient competitor that can

beat democracy at its home game"—providing for everyone's needs better than a democracy could. China is a good example of this: both its proponents and its detractors say that with machine learning and ubiquitous surveillance, China is creating a sustainable autocracy, capable of solving the "basic authoritarian dilemma": "gathering and collating information and being sufficiently responsive to its citizens' needs to remain stable." But Farrell speculates that this isn't actually what's happening—China is actually incredibly unstable (wildcat strikes, unstoppable pro-democracy movements, concentration camps, debt bubbles, manufacturing collapse, routine kidnappings, massive corruption, etc.).[171]

The liberal West has found a better use of digital control: networked democracy that some have called "surveillance capitalism," where democracy and freedom are tolerated but rendered inefficient. This new form of digital control makes it clear why people also rebel in liberal democracies: they don't rebel against freedom, they rebel against what their daily experience tells them—that networked democracy is in some sense even more oppressive than networked authoritarianism.

It is a commonplace today to emphasize the "miraculous" nature of the fall of the Berlin Wall thirty years ago. It was like a dream come true, the realization of something unimaginable, something that wasn't considered possible only a couple of months earlier: the disintegration of the Communist regimes, which collapsed like a house of cards. And who in Poland could have imagined free elections with Lech Wałęsa as president? However, one should add that an even greater "miracle" happened only a couple of years later in 1995: the return of the

---

171 Cory Doctorow, "Networked Authoritarianism May Contain the Seeds of Its Own Undoing," BoingBoing, November 25, 2019, https://boingboing. net/2019/11/25/mote-in-the-cctvs-eye.html.

ex-Communists to power through free democratic elections, within which Wałęsa was totally marginalized and much less popular than General Wojciech Jaruzelski, who, a decade and half earlier, crushed Solidarity with the military coup d'état. Two decades later came the third surprise: Poland is now in the grip of rightist populists who reject both Communism and liberal democracy . . . So what went on here, what led to these unexpected reversals?

One might be tempted to explain this in terms of "capitalist realism," where the problem was simply that East Europeans didn't possess a realistic image of capitalism and were full of immature utopian expectations. The morning after the enthusiasm of the drunken days of victory, people had to sober up and undergo a painful process of learning the rules of the new reality—the price paid for political and economic freedom. It is as if the European Left had to die twice: first as the "totalitarian" Communist Left, then as the moderate democratic Left which, from the 1990s on, has been gradually losing ground.

However, things are a little bit more complex. When people protested against the Communist regimes in Eastern Europe, what the large majority had in mind was not capitalism. They wanted social security, solidarity, a rough kind of justice; they wanted the freedom to live their lives outside of state control, to come together and talk as they pleased; they wanted a life of simple honesty and sincerity, liberated from primitive ideological indoctrination and the prevailing cynical hypocrisy . . . In short, the vague ideals that led the protesters were, to a large extent, taken from socialist ideology itself. And, as we learned from Freud, what is repressed returns in a distorted form. In Europe, the socialism repressed in the dissident imaginary returned in the guise of Right populism.

In his interpretation of the fall of East European Communism, Jürgen Habermas proved to be the ultimate Left Fukuyamist, silently accepting that the existing liberal-democratic order is the best one possible, and that, while we should strive to make it more just, we should not challenge its basic premises. This is why he welcomed precisely what many leftists saw as the big deficiency of the anti-Communist protests in Eastern Europe: the fact that these protests were not motivated by any new visions of the post-Communist future. As he put it, the Central and Eastern European revolutions were just "rectifying" or "catch-up" revolutions, their aim being to enable those societies to gain what the western Europeans already possessed; in other words, to return to the West European normality.

However, the *gilets jaunes,* the Hong Kong protests, and other similar protests today (in Spain, in South Korea, and elsewhere . . .) are definitely *not* catch-up movements. They embody the weird reversal that characterizes today's global situation. The old antagonism between "ordinary people" and financial-capitalist elites is back with a vengeance, with "ordinary people" erupting in protest against the elites, who are accused of being blind to their suffering and demands. However, what is new is that the populist Right has proved to be much more adept in channeling these eruptions in its direction than the Left. Alain Badiou was thus fully justified to say apropos the *gilets jaunes: "Tout ce qui bouge n'est pas rouge"*—all that moves (makes unrest) is not red. Today's populist Right participates in a long tradition of popular protests that were predominantly leftist. Some revolts today can even be considered a case of what are sometimes called revolts of the rich—remember that Catalonia is, together with the Basque Country, the richest part of Spain, and that Hong Kong is per capita much richer than China.

Here, then, is the paradox we have to confront: the populist disappointment at liberal democracy is the proof that 1989 was not just a catch-up revolution. The protests that led to the downfall of the Communist regimes aimed at more than the liberal-capitalist normality, and it was the populist new Right which succeeded in capturing this deeper discontent with capitalist modernity. Freud spoke about *Unbehagen in der Kultur*, the discontent or unease in culture; today, thirty years after the fall of the Wall, the ongoing new wave of protests in liberal democracies themselves (whose exemplary case is the *gilets jaunes* in France) bears witness to a kind of *Unbehagen* in liberal capitalism, and the key question is: Who will be most salient in the articulation of this discontent? Will it be left to nationalist populists to exploit it? Therein resides the big task of the Left: to translate the brewing discontent into a viable program of change.

In the final scene of *V for Vendetta*, thousands of unarmed Londoners wearing Guy Fawkes masks march toward the Houses of Parliament. Without orders, the military allows the crowd to enter, and the people take over . . . OK, a nice ecstatic moment, but I am ready to sell my mother into slavery in order to see *V for Vendetta Part 2*— what would happen the day after the victory of the people, when the ecstatic passion is over and daily life resumes? How would they (re) organize daily life?

Thomas Piketty provides one answer to this question in *Capital and Ideology*, where he proposes a radicalized social democracy.[172] Piketty's proposal is to re-implement and radicalize the welfare state—not to nationalize all wealth as in Soviet-style Communism but to maintain capitalism and redistribute assets by giving every adult a lump sum of money at the age of twenty-five. The progressive income taxes he proposes would allow governments to give everyone a basic income equivalent to 60 percent of the average wage in wealthy nations and cover the costs of decarbonizing the economy. Furthermore, employees should have 50 percent of the seats on company boards; the voting power of even the largest shareholders should be capped

---

172 Piketty is right to emphasize ideology, which plays a key role in society even in an age that praises itself as post-ideological. But Piketty's focus on ideology is all too naïve—he understands it in a quite literal way, arguing that it was possible for the Left to go further in implementing a social-democratic welfare state, but that, from 1970s onwards, it missed this chance due to ideological blindness.

at 10 percent; and we should implement an individualized carbon tax using a personalized card that would track each person's contribution to global heating . . . But what if the rich don't want to pay these confiscatory tax rates and decide to emigrate? Piketty proposes an exit tax and a global justice system that makes it impossible to hide from expropriation anywhere. To that end, he imagines a supranational parliament comprised of members drawn from national legislatures.

The two extremes of the deadlock of today's radical Left are best exemplified by a long substantial TV dialogue between Piketty and Alain Badiou.[173] Badiou's vision is that of the nomadic proletarian emerging as a new global revolutionary force beyond the nation-state and parliamentary democracy, abolishing capitalism. For Badiou, we should step beyond democracy as we know it, into a new revolutionary internationalism. Piketty's proposal is no less utopian, although it presents itself as pragmatic, looking for a solution within the framework of capitalism and democratic procedures.

There is a third dream, that of rejuvenated local democracy, which is, I think, if anything even worse than the proposals of Piketty and Badiou. Today's practices of "direct democracy," from favelas to the "postindustrial" digital culture, have to rely on a state apparatus. Their survival relies on a thick texture of "alienated" institutional mechanisms: Where do electricity and water come from? Who guarantees the rule of law? To whom do we turn for health care? . . . The more a community is self-ruling, the more this network has to function smoothly and invisibly. Maybe we should change the goal of emancipatory struggles from overcoming alienation to enforcing the right kind of alienation—how to achieve the smooth functioning of the "alienated" (invisible) social mechanisms that sustain the space of "non-alienated" communities? This is what makes the welfare state

173 See "Contre Courant – Avec Thomas Piketty," QG TV, November 18 2019, https://www.youtube.com/watch?v=roNWZwo0lS4.

so attractive: I don't have to help the poor myself, the anonymous state apparatus does it for me, allowing me to avoid confronting the excluded and underprivileged face to face.

So, again, why do I still cling to the cursed name of Communism, when I know that the twentieth-century communist project failed, giving birth to new forms of murderous terror? Let me begin with the fact that we live in an age permeated by apocalyptic prospects—there is a multiplicity, a true antinomy of apocalyptic threats. A proviso: when I talk about apocalyptic threats, I am fully aware of how ambiguous and tricky this domain is, and that only a thin line separates accurate perceptions of real dangers from fantasy-scenarios of the global catastrophe that awaits us. There is a specific enjoyment of living in the end time, of awaiting a catastrophe, and the paradox is that it is precisely by fixating on the forthcoming catastrophe that we avoid really confronting it. And I take Communism not as a solution to our woes, but as (still) the best name that enables us to grasp properly the problems we face today and to envisage a way out.

We are at an interesting moment of reversal that Hegel would have rejoiced in. In the last decade or two, the Fukuyamaist "end of history" (where we already have the best possible social formation) turned into its apocalyptic version—we are not yet at the end of history, but we are approaching the end in the guise of an apocalyptic catastrophe . . . There is a formal feature that remains the same in both versions of "the end": the sense of an infinite dragging-on. Fukuyama's world is one in which nothing great or new happens, life just goes on with local ameliorations (the world described decades ago by Kojeve as the world of snobbery); and the apocalypse, too, is always almost here, as we drag on in a kind of endless limbo, the end of time experienced as the impossibility of end(ing). We are used to such a situation in art (which has been dying for over a century) and philosophy (which has from Hegel onward been renouncing itself, overcoming itself). In both

Slavoj Žižek

cases, death leads to extraordinary productivity and the proliferation of new forms, as if the truth of death is a weird immortality.

The only consequent thing to do here is to turn the entire perspective around: the end has already happened, we just didn't notice it. We are like the cat in the old cartoon-joke who walks above a precipice and falls down only when it notices there is no ground under its feet. Our starting point should be that, in some sense, the apocalypse has already happened: our societies are already extensively digitally surveilled and controlled, changes in our environment are already in process, millions are already on the move. We should therefore leave behind the metaphor of it being "five minutes to noon," our last chance to act and prevent the catastrophe. It is already five minutes *past* noon, and the question is what to do in a totally new global constellation. This, of course, doesn't mean we shouldn't fight to prevent the catastrophes awaiting us. To return to the cartoon-joke, our present situation is somewhere between two ends, the first end being that which occurs when we begin to walk without the ground under our feet, and the second end being that which occurs when we actually fall down. We are already walking above the precipice, we've lost the ground beneath our feet, but—in contrast to the cat—the only way *not* to fall to our deaths is to look down into the precipice and act accordingly.

As Alenka Zupančič perspicuously noted, the ultimate proof that the ecological apocalypse has already happened is that it has already been renormalized. Increasingly, we are "rationally" reflecting on how to accommodate ourselves to it and even to profit from it (we read that large parts of Siberia will be open to agriculture; that they can already grow vegetables on Greenland; that the melting of ice on the northern pole will make transport of goods from China to the United States much shorter . . .). An exemplary case of normalization is the predominant reaction to the disclosures of whistleblowers like Assange, Manning, and Snowden, which is not so much denial

("WikiLeaks is spreading lies!") but something like: "We all know our governments are doing these things all the time, there is no surprise here!" The shock at the revelations is thus neutralized by reference to the wisdom of those who are strong enough to sustain a sober look at the realities of life . . . Against such "realism," we should allow ourselves to be fully and naïvely struck by the obscenity and horror of the crimes disclosed by WikiLeaks. Sometimes, naivety is the greatest virtue.

The main voices of renormalization are so-called "rational optimists" like Matt Ridley who bombard us with good news: the 2010s were the best decade in human history, poverty is declining in Asia and Africa, pollution is decreasing, etc.[174] If this is the case, then where does the growing atmosphere of apocalypse come from? Is it not an outgrowth of a self-generated pathological need for unhappiness? When rational optimists tell us that we are overly scared about minor problems, our answer should be that, on the contrary, we are not scared enough. As Alenka Zupančič formulates the paradox: "Apocalypse has already begun, but it seems that we still *prefer to die* than to allow the apocalyptic threat to scare us to death."[175] Moments of doom and resigned expectation of the end are interchanged with pseudo-courageous endurance ("we'll somehow get through it, just don't lose your nerve and fall into panic").

It is easy to see here how rational optimists and prophets of doom are two sides of the same coin: the first are telling us that we can relax, there is no cause for alarm, things are not so bad at all; the others are telling us that everything is already lost and we can just relax and perversely enjoy the spectacle. They both prevent us from

---

174 See Matt Ridley, "We've Just Had the Best Decade in Human History. Seriously," the *Spectator*, December 29, 2019, https://www.spectator.co.uk/2019/12/weve-just -had-the-best-decade-in-human-history-seriously/.

175 Alenka Zupančič, *The Apocalypse Is Still Disappointing* (manuscript).

thinking and acting, from deciding and making a choice. For all of the reasons explained in this book, the best name for this choice is still Communism. It is not that Communism is one of the possible choices; it is the *only* choice. Other choices offered to us (like the "great reset" advocated by big corporations) are just ways to change something so that nothing will really change. Once we choose Communism, we'll realize we *had* to choose it. With Communism, we freely choose what we have to do, what is necessary to do. This is what the old Hegelian claim that freedom is a recognized necessity amounts to: it is not that Communism inevitably has to happen—it might not happen, we might end in a self-destructive orgy or in a neo-feudal corporate capitalism—but once we choose it, we see it's the only way out.

Slavoj Žižek is one of the most prolific and well-known philosophers and cultural theorists in the world today. His inventive, provocative body of work mixes Hegelian metaphysics, Lacanian psychoanalysis, and Marxist dialectic in order to challenge conventional wisdom and accepted verities on both the Left and the Right.